SPANISH

FILM DIRECTORS (1950-1985):

21 PROFILES

by
Ronald Schwartz

The Scarecrow Press, Inc.
Metuchen, N.J., & London
1986

Library of Congress Cataloging in Publication Data

Schwartz, Ronald, 1937-
   Spanish film directors (1950-1985).

   Bibliography: p.
   Includes index.
   1. Moving-pictures--Spain--History.   2. Moving-picture
plays--History and criticism.   3. Moving-picture
producers and directors--Spain.   I. Title.
PN1993.5.S7S3   1986   791.43'0233'0922   85-8287
ISBN 0-8108-1818-3

DEDICATION

For José Luis Borau,
with affection and esteem
because of his love for cinema
and the Spanish film industry.

CONTENTS

ACKNOWLEDGMENTS

The writing of a film book involves viewing hundreds of films. I am especially grateful and indebted to the following institutions and individuals on both sides of the Atlantic:

In New York to: (1) the Museum of Modern Art Film Center, especially Charles Silver and Ron Magliozzi; (2) the staff of the Lincoln Center Library for the Performing Arts; and (3) the American Film Institute in Washington, D. C. and Los Angeles, California.

In Madrid to: (1) the entire staff of the Filmoteca Nacional whose Chief, Luis García Berlanga and Administrative Assistant Florentino Soria extended me every courtesy. Also at the Filmoteca, I owe much to the guidance of Serrano de Osma (a great Spanish film director himself of the 1940s) for his help with securing prints and viewing with me many of the films described within these pages. Manuel de Soria provided me with many of the stills that appear in this book. Chief Librarian Dolores Devisa and her assistants Alicia Potes and Asunción Baraña Cid were most helpful in the retrieval of printed information and the use of Xerox facilities in the Filmoteca's small but well-run Library. The Filmoteca's projectionists, José Luis Fernández and Felipe Flores helped me experience the Spanish cinema under the best viewing conditions possible. José Luis at the Alphaville Bookstore provided much guidance in securing stills and out of print books and magazines. Finally, José Luis Borau, a great film director and sincere friend, gave me inspiration and provided contacts with directors, actors, actresses and film critics so that I could complete this volume.

I am also indebted to the PSC-CUNY Research Foundation for two travel grants which made researching this project entirely possible. I am also grateful to many people at Kingsborough Community College, especially my Chairperson, Dr. Julio Hernández-Miyares, who has always been supportive

vii

of my writing and research, and also Dr. Charles Jacobs, Distinguished Professor of Music at CUNY, who has always been genuinely interested in my research and career. The Library Staff at Kingsborough also deserves much praise, especially John Clune, Florence Houser, Sharad Kharkanis, Adele Schneider and Angelo Tripicchio, professionals all, who have contributed to the formation of ideas and shaped the direction of my research in this book as well as several others.

Finally, I must thank my wonderful wife, Amelia, who has graciously encouraged the research, writing, editing and publication of yet another volume of criticism about the land we both love--Spain, and also my son, Jonathan, who is aware of my self-imposed exile while writing and is still supportive of my research. Bless you both.

PREFACE

The idea for this book began in the mid-1970s when I first taught a university course entitled Spanish Cinema. Except for the films of Luis Buñuel and Carlos Saura, most American film distributors had few films by "other" Spanish directors for rental in their catalogues. An occasional Bardem or Berlanga film furtively crossed the Atlantic to New York "art house" cinemas but received little attention. This project then, to present essays on virtually every Spanish film director of importance since 1950 (and known to American audiences), went through numerous phases and changes over the past ten years, but the final product is not too wide of its original mark.

The "original" concept was to present a view of Spanish cinema from the 1950s to the present, citing the best ten leading directors of the period 1950-1975. No attempt has been made to encompass the entire period of Spanish cinema since 1900. Nevertheless, the period I chose was extended from 25 to 35 years of Spanish cinema and the number of film directors studied and included doubled to twenty. Because of two travel grants, I was able to spend the summers of 1981 and 1982 in and around Madrid, interviewing directors, viewing hundreds of films at the Filmoteca Nacional and accumulating whole volumes of valuable information on Spanish cinema from 1900 to the present. What began as a book on several very famous film directors could have also evolved into a history of modern Spanish cinema, from 1950 to the present, a possible successor to the present volume.

For the most part then, Spanish Film Directors (1950-1985) is a larger work than originally intended, limited to a 35-year period which reflects, for me, the mainstream of Spanish cinema, but makes no claims to exhaustiveness. The choice of directors interviewed is personal and the films viewed represent my choices and mine alone. Excluded from this volume are Spanish directors whose careers began before 1950 and who may have influenced the careers of every director

ix

described in this volume. Most notably excluded is Luis Buñuel (see the Afterword) who has been written about extensively and always deserves a book in his own right. Buñuel's "career," however, is more international than Spanish, his cinematic prowess having extended beyond the frontiers of Spain into France, Mexico and the United States. Also excluded were some interesting directorial "careers" of filmmakers who directed only one or two pictures. Spanish Film Directors (1950-1985) limits itself to films produced and directed in the Iberian peninsula, sound films of feature length, and live action film, with occasional forays into the areas of documentary and "experimental" films; but, as a rule, makers of short subjects and animated films have not been included.

With these admittedly important limitations, I believe this volume to be quite thorough, although it may not be as complete as one may ideally wish. On one level, it may be considered an A to Z of Spanish film directors. However, it is much more than that. It is a first attempt in hardcover to give recognition to men and women in the Spanish film industry and the first comprehensive volume of its kind for American readers. There has been only one previous published work on the subject: Vicente Molina Foix's New Cinema in Spain, a paperback monograph published by the British Film Institute in 1977. The entries regarding directors were rather short, capsule evaluations rather than full-length essays. I have attempted to expand and utilize my own interviews to add further personal dimensions to the life and work of all Spanish film directors under consideration. Much like Andrew Sarris, the leading film critic of the Village Voice, I have always affirmed an "auteurist" approach to film criticism. Spanish "auteurism" exists among all the directors I interviewed since each "personality" took serious responsibility for what appeared on the screen; they are personalities who shape their work more intentionally than not. In sum, this book can be considered a critical study of various types of artistic temperaments, directors who design their work exclusively for the cinema. And each Spanish film director is a "personality" in his own right, as the reader will discover in the course of perusing and using this volume.

Ronald Schwartz
Professor of Romance Languages
City University of New York
New York City
April 1985

NOTES ON FILMOGRAPHIES & PHOTOS

At the beginning of each chapter, I have listed for each director whose work is analyzed in depth in this volume all the feature films on which he or she received a screen credit as director, as well as some additional relevant information.

Since filmographies are often inaccurate, I relied mostly on primary source materials--the actual screen credits themselves and press books given to me by each director. I have not simply taken credits already compiled from secondary sources (which are often inaccurate) but have relied on the directors themselves, as well as the library and files of the Museum of Modern Art in New York City and the Filmoteca Nacional in Madrid. The objective was not only to list the correct titles for each director, but to list each film as it probably appeared on the screen.

The reader should also note that titles translated into English from the original are the most popular and best known feature films of the director and have probably received extensive showing internationally.

Also, with the exception of the photographs and stills in Chapter 18 (Antoni Ribas), for which credit is given to Romi Montané, Barcelona, Spain, 1982, all remaining photos of Spanish film directors were taken by the author and all other stills were given to me for use in this volume by the directors themselves or by permission of the Filmoteca Nacional (Madrid), whose archivist, Manuel de Soria, Director of Film Stills & Archives, acknowledges permission. Besides these permissions, I must acknowledge for posterity the remarks of my publisher: "What's a film book without photos or stills?"

INTRODUCTION

Spanish Film Directors (1950-1985) began as an idea
for a volume in the mid-1970s. By the time serious research began in the early 1980s, the American Film Institute
under Michael Webb's direction mounted a show of some fifteen Spanish films which circulated for one year throughout
major cities in the United States and Canada, beginning at
New York City's Beacon Theatre. Webb contended that "for
thirty-five years, following the Civil War (1936-39), the
Spanish Cinema was under tight control, subject to censorship by state and church."[1] Nevertheless, several directors
like Bardem, Berlanga and Buñuel could defy restrictions
and make occasional personal statements rooted in their realistic worlds. New Spanish Cinema was born as a protest
over General Francisco Franco's censorship policies.

When Franco's rule and health declined in the mid-
1970s, censorship was abolished and with this development
was born a new, exciting cinema. Formerly taboo subjects
--sexuality, the church, the army, the Civil War, use of
narcotics--were openly explored. The Spanish cinema was
no longer escapist and entertaining but, at long last, realistically mirrored the society it depicted in its films. "The
new freedom brought license, and a liberation of previously
repressed talent: a dangerous yet exhilarating mixture of
art and militancy."[2] English critic Roger Mortimore of
Sight & Sound also noted the Spanish cinema's new lease on
life with Franco's death in 1975. He recalls, "While the
bulk of films of the Second Republic continued to be kitsch
(bandits, bullfighters and gypsies), there were some that be-
tokened awareness of social and political realities."[3] When
Franco came to power in 1939, he ushered in a revival of the
Hollywood "state-supported cinema of white telephone comedies and films in praise of the armed forces."[4] It was some
thirty-five years later before the Spanish film industry could
pry itself free of the Franco-inspired cinema of frock-coat
dramas, historical tableaux and religious kitsch. Beginning
with 1975, the majority of film directors treated in this vol-

ume have gone other ways since Franco's death--thematically and financially. There is greater cooperation between the television industry and film production companies. Spain still faces a problem in the distribution of films nationally and internationally.

It should be noted that two Spanish films, El nido (The Nest, 1981) by Jaime de Armiñán and Volver a empezar (To Begin Again, 1982) by José Luis Garcí, were both Academy Award contenders in the Foreign Language Film category and Garcí's film took the prize, assuring Twentieth Century-Fox a financial success and the film international recognition and distribution. Indeed, Spanish cinema has traveled a long road for recognition, as have some of the directors cited in this volume. Although these filmmakers are considered alphabetically, Bardem and Berlanga really belong chronologically to the 1950s. They continue to produce and direct films into the 1980s, but unlike Buñuel, no film critic has accorded them the status of a single volume of research in English. All the other film directors mentioned in this volume, somewhat "younger" directors than Bardem and Berlanga who promote and support what may be called "new" Spanish Cinema, have enjoyed fruitful careers between 1960 and the present.

Chapter 1

ALVARO DEL AMO (1942)

Filmography

Shorts

1968--Preparaciones; 1972--Jugo; 1974--Paisaje con árbol;
1978--Cuento; 1979--Presto agitato

Features

1979--Dos (Two); 1980--El Tigre

Alvaro del Amo was born in Madrid in 1942. He
studied for a career in law but later went to Spain's Official
School of Cinema where he made his first film in black and
white, Preparations, in 1968. As with his first venture into
writing a story, Amo usually prepares his own script and
directs every one of his productions personally. All of his
subsequent films until now have been shot in black and white
except for Paisaje con árbol (Landscape with Tree) in 1974,
filmed in color. Happily married and the father of one
daughter called Yolanda, Amo is also a film critic and has
written for Nuestro cine, Primer acto and El viejo topo
among other leading magazines. He has also co-produced
a series of books on plays and written prologues and translations for nearly sixty plays published in this series. His
translations of plays are too numerous to cite, as are the
titles of prologues and original screenplays he has written
for other film directors. However, three plays, two novels
and two books of criticism are worthy of mention, particularly the latter two since they deal with film criticism:
Film & the Criticism of Film (1971) and the only study on
filmed plays from the Spanish stage, Comedia cinematografía
española, which is his most successful critical volume to

1

Alvaro del Amo with actor Fernando Rey (photo courtesy of the director).

date.   Amo continues to be a prolific writer of film criticism when he is not filming his own screenplays.

Amo made his first film, Dos (1979), on a shoestring budget of some two hundred thousand pesetas in about five days.   Like other "new cinema" directors in Spain, he is interested in creating a "personal" cinema, one that is intellectually oriented, a cinema for the elite, not the masses. [1]   Obviously he cannot earn a living at elitist cinema and so works in Spanish television, dubbing soundtracks, and also continues his writing of film criticism, which pays him a small but steady salary.   When he began filming Dos, he originally envisaged it as a two-character play. [2]

Dos is a very short film, running some 75 minutes. It deals with a married couple who like to play games in their apartment--word games and riddles--tell stories, give passwords, trade dolls and, above all, dance and dance and dance and go around and around and around as if their dance is a metaphor for the circular, enclosed, hermetic, airless world that is their apartment, their life together.   The camera, which never moves out of their apartment, swirls

around the actors as they move through the events of the
scenario. Julia and Luis are, at the same time, lovers,
children, cousins, parents, brothers, daughters, a couple.
They continually speak about an infinity of "things." They
hand one another dolls, candies, scarves, and while they
are doing this, so-called "intimate revelations" of their love
(and hate) of each other take place. From their continuous
dialogue there emerge several different roles played by each
character. Luis appears to be a priest at times and Julia,
a mother in search of a child. As the film speeds to its
conclusion, we find the couple retreating back into their bed
as the camera tracks backwards out through the blinds of
their apartment window where it had entered in the film's
opening shot some seventy minutes before.

Exaggeratedly intense bright lighting tends to give the
black and white film many hues of grey in its apartment setting. Every scene appears to be shot twice. Dos is a chilling experience, perhaps pseudo-intellectual, snobbish, re-
petitive, even dull at times. Nevertheless, Amo tries val-
iantly to create a "new" Spanish cinema never before seen
on local Madrid screens. He has the courage to experiment,
and Dos is a film of the most avant-garde, intended for a
very, very limited audience. Dos has the power to irritate
its viewers, or, in certain cases, put them to sleep. One
feels, at times, that film critics should concentrate on their
writing and not jump into filmmaking. Of course, if François Truffaut continued to write for Cahiers du cinéma, we
would never have experienced the power and depth of his
marvelous directorial talent. And so it is with Alvaro del
Amo. His films are purely intellectual experiences, but with
little real magic. Intellect is not enough to carry a film to
its successful conclusion. Even though Amo acknowledges
the influence of Harold Pinter upon his work and Roger
Mortimore sees "the leitmotif of a dance between scenes
[which] gives the film the structure of a rondo,"[3] Dos remains nothing more than an experimental piece of cinema.

Amo is probably one of the most "uncommercial" directors living in Spain today and deals in an extremely elitist, personal cinema. Yet Amo's films may find a small
audience where none existed before. His type of experimen-
tation was never encouraged in Spain in earlier years. The
"experimental film" of the Seventies is something new aesthetically in Spain. It is also one of the most striking examples because of its "austere, frozen beauty which Amo
himself calls a sad and petrified beauty."[4] The personality

Two stills from <u>Dos</u>--Joaquín Hinojosa and Isabel Mestres.

of the director (or his unobtrusive direction) is very much in evidence and is greatly aided by the frigid, piercing photography of Angel Luis Fernández, who, like Teo Escamilla, is one of Spain's newly discovered talented cinematographers, having also worked with other directors such as Trueba, Colomo and Zulueta.

Dos represents a new direction for Spanish cinema. It was made by a group of "friends" or "angels" on an insignificant budget. The actors, Joaquín Hinojosa and Isabel Mestres, received no salary for Amo's first feature film. His second feature, El Tigre (The Tiger) showed briefly in 1980 and also received minor acclaim. Amo continues to write criticism, work in Spanish television and at times act in some of his own plays and films. Only time will tell if his experimental, personal and elitist vision will attract the Spanish public and bring him the acclaim for which he continually searches.

Bibliography

"Alvaro del Amo." Contracampo: Revista del cine No. 19 (Feb. 1981), 13-22.

V. Ponce. "Once para Dos." Contracampo No. 19 (Feb. 1981), 11.

Chapter 2

JAIME DE ARMIÑAN (1927)

Filmography

1969--Carola de día, Carola de noche; 1971--Mi querida señorita (My Dearest Señorita); 1973--Un casto varón español; 1974--El amor del Capitán Brando; 1975--Jo, papá; 1977--Nunca es tarde, Ursula; 1978--Al servicio de la mujer española; 1980--El nido (The Nest); 1981--En septiembre; 1984--Stico.

Like Alvaro del Amo, Jaime de Armiñán was born in Madrid, on March 9, 1927 into a family of writers and politicians, and also received a Law degree. A prolific writer, he worked as a critic for several Spanish magazines and is the author of several plays, the most famous of which are Eva sin manzana (Eve without an Apple) and Nuestro fantasma (Our Ghost), both national prize winners, in 1953 and 1956 respectively. He began working in Spanish television in the late fifties, turning out some fifteen TV scripts, and received several awards. Most notably, in 1968, he won a prize for his musical satire on Spanish censorship entitled Stories of Frivolity.

By 1970, Armiñán turned to motion pictures and his third feature film, Mi querida señorita, was nominated for an Academy Award in the Best Foreign Film category in the United States in 1973. Coincidentally, his El amor del Capitán Brando took second prize at the Berlin Film Festival. His best film to date, El nido, was also nominated for an Academy Award in 1981. Armiñán is a prolific writer-director and continues to write the scripts for his own films. He has directed since the early 1970s.

Jaime de Armiñán projects the appearance of a very

thoughtful person. Before filming any project he first must like the story, and he usually takes six weeks to completely film an entire feature. He never attended film school and claims his success is due to using theatrical methods in film. He rehearses all his actors before shooting and is especially fond of using children in his films. In fact, his son appeared in El amor del Capitán Brando and Ana Torrent, the sensational child star of Victor Erice's Spirit of the Beehive, appears as Armiñán's teenage protagonist in El nido. When asked about his own films, Armiñán claims to be a "free cinematic soul. Rehearsing does not always work. In fact, Ana Torrent is a better actress when she is placed before the camera unrehearsed. She projects a luminous quality that is sometimes lost if there is too much rehearsal."[1]

Armiñán believes his films reflect his own feelings about Spanish life but he is generally worried about the current state of Spanish cinema. Although he has won several prestigious awards, he feels the Spanish film industry is on the wane and is always besieged by distribution and investment problems. According to Armiñán, it currently costs some 30 million pesetas (about $\frac{1}{4}$-million dollars) to produce a film in Spain. Regarding his pre-Franco productions, he was surprised that Mi querida señorita was produced at all and even more surprised that it was left virtually untouched by the censors in 1973. "One scene was cut ... of a prostitute who appeared semi-nude. After Franco's death, you could have total nudity on the screen and the censors would let it pass today."[2] Armiñán usually does his scenes in one take, rarely more, because, he says, it is too expensive to film retakes. When I last spoke with Armiñán, he was on his way to Mexico City to film a Spanish Western there, a genre he had never attempted before.

Jaime de Armiñán is best known in the United States and Spain for two feature films: Mi querida señorita and El nido. My Dearest Señorita (1971) stars one of Spain's most famous leading men, José Luis López Vásquez, and deals directly with the theme of bi-sexuality. Vásquez first plays Adela, a spinster who lives quietly alone in an isolated provincial Spanish town. With no other accomplishments of a "lady of rank" and a small annuity, she spends her days sewing and doing charity work. Never feeling particularly attracted to men, she is waited upon in her home by a faithful lady's maid who adores her. One day, the local manager of a bank starts to court Adela and sets his sights on marriage.

Above and opposite, four stills of José Luis López Vásquez in <u>Mi querida señorita</u> (1971).

Adela, repelled by the physical contact of her suitor and
after an argument with her faithful servant over the situation,
resolves to consult a doctor. (The gynecologist is played by
another actor-director, José Luis Borau, who is also the
producer of this film.) Adela discovers after consultation
that, after all, she is not a woman.

After several therapy sessions, "Juan" arrives in
Madrid and meets the servant girl he fired when he was
"Adela." Juan searches for work and a new purpose in life
with his new identity. Life is very hard in Madrid and Juan
used his sewing skills to bring him a small income and en-
able him to obtain a work permit. However, he has problems
securing an identity card. As Juan prospers, he falls in
love with Isabelita (the servant girl) but denies himself con-
summation of their affair for fear of a poor sexual response.
The film proceeds to its predictable conclusion: Juan is able
to fulfill his duties as a man and is marvelously successful
with Isabelita. While making love to her, he warns that one
day he will tell her a "secret." In their intimacy, Isabelita
sometimes calls her lover "Juan" and sometimes "Adelita."
The implication is that Isabelita had known for some time
about "Juan's" bisexuality. My Dearest Señorita is an extremely witty film played with high style and directed with
careful, exquisite taste. The film was selected by the
American Film Institute for its "New Spanish Cinema" series
which circulates throughout the United States and Canada.

Armiñán's other successful film to reach American
audiences is The Nest (1980). Set in the province of Castille, it is the story of an aging hidalgo (gentleman), Alejandro,
who lives in an ultra-modern but rustic country house near
Salamanca, and his relationship with a girl on the verge of
puberty named Goyita. Alejandro, beautifully played by
Hector Alterio, lives a purposeless life filled by computer
chess, horseback riding, and an elaborate stereo system to
which he conducts to the sounds of Haydn's "Creation." His
wife had apparently died several years earlier and Alejandro
is disposed to meeting the thirteen-year-old village girl
Goyita, also beautifully played by Ana Torrent. Because this
serious, mature and reflective teenager is just as alone as
Alejandro when they meet, she insinuates herself into his
life and a strange, over-powering relationship develops between them, at first Platonic but later with covert sexual
overtones. The older man acts much like a child and later
forbids Goyita to see him. Goyita, the daughter of the local
Civil Guardsman, makes more elaborate demands upon

Poster advertising <u>El nido</u> (1980), Armiñán's best film, nominated for an Academy Award in 1981.

Alejandro as their relationship grows. He balks at first,
then complies by giving her gifts, including his late wife's
clothes. Finally, they swear an oath of allegiance in blood.
She asks Alejandro to avenge her hate for a local Civil Guard
sergeant (her father's superior officer) who killed her pet
hawk. Aware of the love he feels for Goyita, Alejandro lets
her family send her away to an aunt's home in faraway Salamanca. Following Goyita there, Alejandro realizes he must
fulfill the pact and kill the sergeant out of "love" for Goyita.
From high above, on horseback in the mountains, he fires at
the sergeant who is riding with Goyita's father (the latter
wonderfully played by Ovidi Montllor) and is shot dead by
both Civil Guards. He is buried on a hillside on his own
estate. Goyita visits the gravesite and promises never to
give herself sexually to anyone else, a reaffirmation of the
pact they had sworn for eternity.

Ana Torrent ("the Spanish Lolita") and Hector Alterio in
El nido (1980).

The Nest has some especially well-played scenes between Alterio and Torrent--they learn to sing together, lead
an orchestra, hunt for birds, and just play together. Torrent
enacts the role of child-woman with extraordinary charm and
grace. Alterio realizes, although he was once married, that

he had never really lived passionately until he met Goyita
(Torrent). He is doomed to die. For me, the nest is symbolic of a comfortable place, a sanctuary which one finds
only in death. The Nest is an extraordinarily sensitive and
beautiful film. Some American film critics have referred to
Torrent's role as "the Spanish Lolita"[3] and the entire film
as "hermetically sealed hokum,"[4] with fraudulent character-
izations. But most reviewers agree that Ana Torrent has
one of the most remarkable, profoundly affecting faces before the camera. Vincent Canby notes: "She appears to
express everything doing nothing."[5] Although this film
appeared in the early 1980s, it reminded me of films made
before Franco's death, when writers and directors alike, in
order to circumvent censorship, used allegory, understate-
ment, allusions and ellipses, transforming their screenplays into a national cinema style of "possibilities" typical
of only Spain during this repressive era. Although El nido
reminds me of this era of multiple possibilities and indirect
disclosure, its ambiguity is executed with such purposeful
good taste that Armiñán has preserved his reputation as a
careful, lyrical story-teller and filmmaker. One hopes he
will continue to film unusual stories of ordinary or extraordinary behavior with the sensitivity, charm and psychological acuity he had already demonstrated in dealing with
somewhat controversial themes.

Thus far, most of Armiñán's films have shown strong
literary and theatrical influences, as a result perhaps of his
apprenticeship in the early 1970s as a TV-scriptwriter turned
film director. With El nido, we see emerging a new kind
of originality in the execution of his themes, a possible
yearning for commercial success which was not apparent in
his earlier films.

Bibliography

Ansen, David. "Review of El nido." Newsweek (Aug. 30,
1982), 62.

Besa, Peter. "Review of Nunca es tarde." Variety (Oct. 26,
1977), 20.

Besa, Peter. "Review of El nido." Variety (Oct. 8, 1980),
22.

Besa, Peter. "Review of En septiembre." Variety (Apr.
12, 1982), 18.

Besa, Peter. "Review of En septiembre." Casablanca (Apr. 16, 1982), 53.

Besa, Peter. "Review of El nido." Variety (Aug. 4, 1982), 18.

Besa, Peter. "Review of Stico." Variety (Dec. 26, 1984), 16.

Canby, Vincent. "Review of El nido: Widower and Girl in The Nest." New York Times (Aug. 10, 1982), 42.

Carroll, Kathleen. "Review of El nido." Daily News (Aug. 9, 1982), 35.

"En montaje: El nido." Cinema 2002 No. 64 (June 1980), 20-21.

Maslin, Janet. "Review of It's Never Too Late." New York Times (June 29, 1984), C, 8.

Chapter 3

JUAN ANTONIO BARDEM (1922)

Filmography

1951--Esa pareja feliz (co-directed with Luis Berlanga);
1953--Cómicos; 1954--Felices pascuas; 1955--Muerte de un
ciclista (Death of a Cyclist); 1956--Calle Mayor (Main Street
or The Lovemaker); 1957--La venganza; 1959--Sonatas; 1960--
A las cinco de la tarde; 1962--Los inocentes; 1963--Nunca
pasa nade (Nothing Ever Happens); 1965--Los pianos mecáni-
cos; 1968--El último día de la guerra; 1970--Varietés; 1971--
La isla misteriosa; 1972--La corrupción de Chris Miller
(The Corruption of Chris Miller); 1975--El poder del deseo;
1976--El puente (The Bridge or The Long Weekend); 1979--
Siete días de enero.

Just as Luis García Berlanga deserves an entire
volume dedicated to his life and films (see Chapter 4), so
does Juan Antonio Bardem. In fact, Bardem and Berlanga
are the two giants of the Spanish film industry who began
their careers in the early 1950s and still continue to turn
out commercially successful films, some of them demanding
international attention more than others.

Juan Antonio Bardem was born in Madrid on June 2, 1922
into a family of actors. He was thirteen years old when Civil War
broke out in Spain and he moved with his family from Madrid to
Barcelona, then to San Sebastian, to Seville and back to Madrid
once again. As a student he majored in Agricultural Engineering
but by 1947 he chose a film career instead and entered Madrid's
film school (Instituto de Investigaciones Cinematográficas--
I. I. E. C.) where he met Luis García Berlanga. Their first
film project collaboration, Esa pareja feliz (That Happy
Couple), was released in 1951. Although Bardem did not
receive his film school diploma because of his "political"

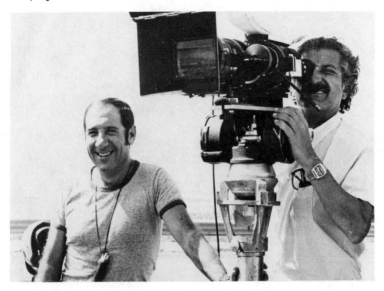

Juan Antonio Bardem (behind camera) with actor Alfredo Landa on the set of El puente (The Bridge).

views, he continued writing scripts and was able to collaborate successfully once again with Berlanga on the latter's Bienvenido Señor Marshall (Welcome Mr. Marshall), preparing a witty script under Berlanga's expert direction. It was an instantaneous hit at the Cannes Film Festival in 1953 and assured productive film careers for both men. Bardem and Berlanga gave a new lease on life to a then failing film industry and provided it with international status when Welcome Mr. Marshall achieved world-wide release. Known as a sincere and stylistically vigorous filmmaker, Bardem expressed the realities of his country better than anyone at that time with the possible exception of Luis Buñuel. He once declared, "An artist cannot transplant his roots; I can speak only of that which I know well: Spain."[1] In his effort to redress a cinema that was "politically ineffective, socially false, intellectually infirm, aesthetically crusty and industrially rickety,"[2] Bardem's first film production apart from Berlanga was Muerte de un ciclista (Death of a Cyclist), probably still considered his best-known film work outside of Spain. With this film, Bardem hoped to create a "national cinema with love, sincerity and honor.... A filmmaker

Lucia Bose and Alberto Closas in Muerte de un ciclista
(Death of a Cyclist, 1955).

cannot hope to change the world ... he must make a contri-
bution ... donate all his efforts to a positive, useful cinema
that will reveal the reality of things so they will change."[3]

The emergence of committed, realistic films from
Franco's Spain aroused wide interest in Bardem's work.   In
1956, while filming Calle mayor with Betsy Blair, he was
imprisoned on "political" charges.   There was a huge international outcry which precipitated his release two weeks
later.   The New York Times reported that he was detained
after clashes between university students and Falangists
(pro-Franco supporters) in Papalencia, a small town north
of Madrid.   He was accused by Falangists of writing a
script for Death of a Cyclist which was alleged to contain
critical overtones about the present regime.   He was cleared
of all charges after eleven days, although Cyclist does contain a student strike scene, a genuine parallel and model for
some students who were seeking university reforms.

Bardem has never been a stranger to adversity, political or otherwise. In 1976, Variety reported that he was jailed--and released once again after seven days--for not paying a fine imposed upon him in a May Day amnesty protest. [5] Apparently a group of film critics in Barcelona sought his release on the grounds that two films, Carlos Saura's Cría cuervos and Ricardo Franco's Pascual Duarte, had just opened in theaters, supposedly representing the "new" democracy or "liberalism" of the Spanish government and it would appear hypocritical to jail a film director for having demonstrated in favor of political amnesty.

The majority of Bardem's films contain some note of political criticism. When he wanted to film a story critical of peasant life in the provinces, originally called Los segadores (The Reapers), the Franco government insisted that its plot be changed; the result was a conventional melodrama which was later called La venganza (Vengeance), whose title was also chosen by the censors. At this point in his career, Bardem founded his own production company, UNINCI, helped to produce Luis Buñuel's controversial anti-Catholic masterpiece, Viridiana, in 1961, and became so embroiled in the political and religious debate over the film that his production company was forced to close down. Making tracks for Argentina, Bardem directed Los inocentes there in 1962 but soon returned to Spain and has remained there ever since. Although he continues his courageous attempts at a realistic and critical examination of Spanish life through his films, even since Franco's death in 1975 Bardem's efforts have missed their target. Bardem is best known internationally for five films: two in his early period--Death of a Cyclist and Main Street; one transitional film, Nothing Ever Happens, made as a Franco-Spanish co-production; and two films from his latest, perhaps most "decadent" period (for want of a better descriptive term), The Corruption of Chris Miller and The Long Weekend). All are worthy of brief discussion in order to demonstrate the trajectory of Bardem's career in Spanish cinema.

Death of a Cyclist, Bardem's most famous, appears on every critic's list of the top ten or fifteen best films from Spain. It tells the story of Juan, a university professor, who, while driving back from a rendezvous with his mistress María-José, accidentally knocks down and kills a cyclist. Panicking, the couple leave the scene, afraid that their clandestine affair will be discovered. When they discover the cyclist's death, Juan tries to convince Maria to

confess to the crime. The latter, unable to give up her
husband, her wealth and societal position, runs down her
lover instead. While leaving the scene she swerves her
car to avoid hitting yet another cyclist, but goes to her own
death, crashing into a ravine. Although the ending of this
film was a bit melodramatic, Bardem was obliged to punish
the adulterous woman (beautifully played by Lucia Bose).
Nevertheless, the film's moral, social and political implications offered a scathing commentary on contemporary
Spanish society of the mid-1950s. When asked what he
would do if he could make a film free of the limitations of
censorship, Bardem once answered, "I firmly believe that
the cinema, if it is to be worth anything at all, has to
bear witness to the reality which surrounds us here and
now. I must make films with each and every one of the
limitations that reality imposes upon me."[6]

Although Death of a Cyclist conveys its social anger
through the medium of a popularly acceptable thriller, the
story of adultery is still conventional. The sub-plots of the
film, however, are more interesting. We learn that Juan
holds his university position through the patronage of in-
fluential rich friends. It is he who foments the student reform movement for better university conditions because he
can no longer tolerate the vulgarity and greed of his own
social set and tries to identify with the simpler values of
life. He envisages his own guilt as part of the wider guilt
of the privileged towards the rest of society. His decision
to surrender to the police suggests self-expiation, a pur-
gation of his own association with a society and class system
he cannot ever hope to change.

Bardem asserts the power of the individual and the
preservation of his dignity in face of a decadent society as
the principal message of the film. However, the "message"
is sometimes obfuscated by Bardem's own lack of continuity
and editing style. Sometimes we feel we do not get close
enough to the characters and sometimes the appearance of
the husband and the lover confuses us because they
look so much alike physically.[7] The two levels of
society--the rich, upper-classes and the poor student popu-
lation of the middle and lower strata--are presented as
extreme opposites. Bardem contrasts the ruthless character of the rich decadents and the banal, thin motivations of
the "good" people who supposedly embody the real values
of the film. Nevertheless, Death of a Cyclist is a superior
effort, in which Bardem reveals in depth the social implications

of the plot, even though his individual characters are cold, bloodless and sacrificed to the trajectory of the narrative.

Most of Bardem's films of the early 1950s ambiguously or obliquely provide social commentary if not profound penetration into the psyches of individual personalities. Calle mayor (The Lovemaker), which followed closely after Cyclist, starred the American actress Betsy Blair as Isabel, a "wallflower" who is the butt of a practical joke. Bardem focuses here on an individual who will suffer as a consequence of the small town in which she lives. A plain spinster of thirty-five living in a small provincial Spanish town (and not even wealthy) is falsely made love to by one of the town's local gigolos and is jilted by him. Juan, the gigolo, is a handsome weakling who obliges the love-smitten spinster only to find that he has a conscience and is striken by the enormity and cruelty of the practical "joke" played on her by the townsmen. In this tender but brutal film, Bardem's spinster becomes a symbol of all the homely, unloved women in the world who wait but never fulfill their dreams. Juan runs off to Madrid at the conclusion and Isabel, still desperately in love, is left to her lonely destiny. Calle mayor is a perceptive portrait of small-town life in contemporary Spain--the señoritos, the rich bored young men searching for their dreary pleasures among the señoritas, the women trapped by their religion and traditions in a male-dominated society.

Calle mayor was filmed in two versions: Spanish and French. At this point in his career, Bardem began searching for an audience beyond the frontiers of Iberia and found one in France. Nothing Ever Happens (1963), like Calle mayor, is critical of Spanish machismo. The object of the criticism this time, is a beautiful blonde French woman admirably played by Corinne Marchand. Forced by an attack of appendicitis to leave a road show traveling through Spain, Jacqueline undergoes surgery and must recuperate in a small provincial Spanish town. The doctor falls in love with his patient. His wife complains bitterly. The French girl becomes a catalyst for all the pent-up desires and emotions felt by spouses, priests, and the local schoolmaster played by Jean-Pierre Cassel. But as the title suggests, nothing ever happens. This is another of those well-made black-and-white films using Cinemascope projection in which Bardem's huge anamorphic lenses captures the small-mindedness of Spaniards in a provincial setting and in which he utilizes bankable, international actors.

Two scenes from Bardem's <u>Nunca pasa nada</u> (<u>Nothing Ever Happens</u>, 1963). Above, Corinne Marchand; below, Jean-Pierre Cassel.

The Corruption of Chris Miller, made in 1972, is
Bardem's first venture into combining Cinemascope and color.
It stars the ill-fated American Jean Seberg as Ruth, a fashion
designer spending her summer in the country with her beautiful, neurotic, over-sexed daughter--played by singing star
Marisol. Although their relationship is one of mutual dis-
trust, a handsome young Englishman played by Barry Stokes
becomes the love object for each woman at different times
throughout the film. The countryside has been terrorized
by a hatchet murderer. Apparently, both women suspect
that the Englishman is the criminal. We also learn that
Seberg's husband is in a psychiatric ward and her daughter
was raped at the local school by a burly body-builder. As
the tension builds, the Englishman makes love to Marisol,
only to be stabbed to death by her. The real murderer is
their neighbor, José-Luis, who is a perfect look-alike for
the Englishman (and the only worthy plot twist in a fairly
predictable film.) The sub-plot, to explain why the Englishman comes on the scene in the first place, is even more
laughable. It seems he was released from an English prison
and sought to discover a cache of jewels hidden by Seberg's
husband, who had stolen them before being committed to an
asylum. Having found the jewels and vowed to stay together,
mother and daughter hide the Englishman's body under a
newly built road.

With this film, Bardem makes a career turnabout of
360 degrees. No longer interested in a "critical" approach
or in revealing character traits or motivations, in Chris
Miller he presents a technicolored, lush picture of Santander
and Northern Spain where the most improbable and sensational events take place, and the screenplay says nothing
trenchant about Spain or Spaniards. In fact, because the
film is such a multi-national co-production with so many
international actors, it loses its Spanish identity. Although
the plot is taut and the acting is all very good, Bardem has
produced an entertainment that tells us very little about himself or his country.

Moving away from the luminous performances of
Lucia Bose, Betsy Blair and Jean Seberg, Bardem turns to
a male star, Alberto Landa, as the centerpiece for El
puente (The Long Weekend). Elaborately over-produced,
once again in Cinemascope and color, the 1976 film begins
with an auto mechanic's desire to take a week's vacation in
Torremolinos with his current girl friend. Traveling by
motor bike, his girl leaves with another group of vacationers

Alfredo Landa (left) and unidentified actor in El puente (The Long Weekend).

instead, leaving Landa quite on his own. Small, hairy, foul-mouthed, funny-looking and pseudo-macho, Landa begins his trek southward and in somewhat picaresque fashion par- ticipates in a series of events: he is picked up in a van by a group of California hippies who cannot find any solace in America (they are critical of the war in Viet Nam, unemploy- ment and the deadly bourgeois life-style in America); he en- counters a young woman, who tells him his hands should be clean and smooth, and subsequently they make love before she leaves him to sleep by a dying fireside on the road; he meets another group of traveling actors who are later jailed because their play is too "liberal"; he encounters a group of Catalonians taking drugs and driving at speeds up to 160 kilometers per hour, and is almost killed in a car wreck. We witness the slow "maturation" of the Landa character on his trip to Spain's Gold Coast. At last, he reaches the Mediterranean but after his brief vacation, he must return to his job and becomes once again just "one of the boys."

Although The Long Weekend is technically very well produced, directed and acted, it is totally a commercial product, not a critical, perceptive or artistic film in any sense like many of Bardem's earlier works. Although Landa plays the mechanic's role in an honest, straightforward manner, his character is two-dimensional, revealing little about his true feelings. After Landa's adventures have been played out, the picaresque entertainments of this film leave very little to ponder. Obviously, Bardem's career has followed a downward trajectory--from artistic endeavor to crass commercialism. He hopes to recoup his international reputation with his newest film, tentatively title Lorca, muerte de un poeta (Lorca, Death of a Poet), which he was filming in 1982-83. Given this serious literary and political subject, once treated in oblique fashion by Jaime Chavarrí in A un Dios desconocido (To an Unknown God), Bardem will now have the chance to film with historical accuracy and literary perception a formerly forbidden subject. In spite of his recent film assignments, one hopes he will be able to re-establish his international reputation and conclusively prove his ability as a director who portrays thoughts and feelings of his fellow Spaniards with transcendence beyond the frontiers of Spain.

Bibliography

Besa, Peter. "Review of Chris Miller." Variety (Aug. 8, 1973), 18.

Besa, Peter. "Review of Siete días de enero." Variety (May 2, 1979), 27.

Canby, Vincent. "Review of Chris Miller." New York Times (Nov. 29, 1979), 39.

Chevallier, J. "Review of Siete días de enero." Image et son (Jan. 1980), 60.

Crowther, Bosley. "Review of Age of Infidelity." New York Times (Aug. 11, 1958), 23.

Falk, Q. "Bardem's Seven Days." Sight & Sound XLVII, 14 (Autumn 1978), 223.

Hawk. "Review of Calle mayor." Variety (Sept. 12, 1956), no page listing, and (Oct. 3, 1956), 26.

Hernández-Les, J. "Review of Siete días de enero." Cinema 2002 (May 1979), 10-19.

Holl. "Review of El Puente." Variety (Aug. 10, 1977), 16.

"Review of Calle mayor." Film-Ideal (Feb. 1957), 29.

"Review of The Lovemaker." Time (May 10, 1958), no page.

"Review of Nunca pasa nada." Film-Ideal (Mar. 1965), 170.

"Review of El puente." Cinema 2002 (Dec. 1976), 48-49.

"Interview with J. A. Bardem." Cinema 2002 (Oct. 1978), 40-44.

Chapter 4

LUIS GARCIA BERLANGA (1921)

Filmography

Short Films: 1948--Paseo por una guerra antigua, Tres cartas; 1949--El circo; 1957--Se vende un tranvía (television).

Full-length Features: 1951--Esa pareja feliz; 1952--Bienvenido Sr. Marshall (Welcome Mr. Marshall); 1953--Novio a la vista; 1956--Calabuch; 1957--Los jueves, milagro; 1961--Plácido; 1962--"La muerte y el Leñador," episode in Las cuatro verdades; 1963--El verdugo (The Executioner or Not on Your Life); 1967--La boutique; 1971--Vivan los novios; 1973--Tamaño natural; 1978--Escopeta nacional (National Shotgun); 1980--Patrimonio nacional (National Trust); 1983--Nacional Tres; 1985--La vaquilla.

Luis García Berlanga, like Juan Antonio Bardem, is one of the most celebrated film directors in Spain, and is the best known internationally. He is considered by many the first auteur of post-Civil War Spanish Cinema and the first to provide it with universal interests that stem from a uniquely personal world. "One starts from a situation in which the individual finds himself with a specific status vis-à-vis the society; for a moment he thinks he will improve but he ends up as he began, if not worse than before."[1] Although the number of films directed by him is small (some ten films in thirty years) because the majority of his projects were blocked by censorship from the Franco regime, Berlanga is still one of the most fascinating directors to emerge in Spain since Luis Buñuel. Unlike the latter, he still works and films there; Buñuel lived and worked mostly abroad. Along with Carlos Saura and Luis Buñuel, Berlanga is the third Spanish film director to be singled out by the International Film Guide to receive extensive critical analysis in

Luis García Berlanga directing a member of the cast on the set of National Trust (1980).

English of his entire career. As in the case of Bardem, a full-length study in English is yet to be attempted about this complex man and the diversity of his films since the early 1950s.

Berlanga was born in Valencia on July 12, 1921 to a family with very liberal political traditions. He read Philosophy and Humanities at the University of Valencia and wrote film criticism while a student there. As a young man during the Civil War, he enlisted with a group of Spanish volunteers. Later, he fought on the Russian front in the famous Blue Division. After World War II, Berlanga returned to his family, now settled in Madrid, and began to write poetry and to paint. He soon found himself writing a collection of erotic books for Editorial Tusquets under the title La sonrisa vertical (The Vertical Smile). He also began to write film scripts as early as 1943. However, influenced by the French culture of the early 1930s and continuing his propensity for the arts and cinema, finally, in 1947 Berlanga decided to enter the National School of Cinema (Instituto de Investigaciones Cinematográficas), just recently formed. He was one of its first graduates along with Bardem and together they co-directed their first commercial film, Esa pareja feliz. Berlanga was in charge of the principal photography and Bardem took charge of the actors.

From the beginning of his career, Berlanga developed a sharp, satirical style. In fact, This Happy Couple was an extremely personal film, dealing with the themes of poverty and the Spanish economic crises of the 1950s, and contrasted significantly with the traditional Spanish films of that era that treated only patriotic, religious or "folkloric" subjects. Berlanga's true genius manifested itself in his lampooning of certain aspects of Spain's political and social worlds, and his hysterical satirizing of certain Spanish foibles did not endear him or his films to the Franco regime. Spanish film critic Vicente Molina-Foix believes both Bardem and Berlanga owe a great debt to the Italian cinema of neo-realism, of Rossellini and Zavattini, since they began to film their own screenplays according to their own ideas of Spanish realism in the culturally impoverished Spain of the early 1950s.[2] Berlanga admits to these influences as well as to that of French director Jacques Becker.[3] In trying to force the Italian neo-realistic cinema on to Spanish subjects, Berlanga successfully produced a series of films known for their picaresque satires of modern Spanish life, but as a result he suffered considerably from political and religious censorship. Although censorship caused him to flee into France on one occasion, Berlanga has finally received the respect and adulation he so rightfully deserved over the past thirty years. Although he directed only fourteen films in that "dark" period, he is now the President of the Filmoteca Nacional and intermittently sits on film juries at international film festivals. His film Escopeta nacional (1978) was probably the most successful commercial film he ever made, taking in over four million dollars in Spain alone that year; it cost one-tenth of that sum to produce.

When I first met Berlanga, a very distinguished grey-haired gentleman, in the summer of 1980, he told me he was a jack-of-all-trades before becoming a filmmaker--a poet, painter, decorator, interested in all of the arts. "I am interested in creating my own myths like Fellini. I am interested in controversy."[4] Rather than discuss his entire film career, Berlanga preferred talking in rambling fashion about a multitude of subjects. In spite of the fact that Escopeta nacional was such a financial success in Spain, he told me it was an extremely personal film and not "international" enough to be shown abroad. He asked if I had seen Welcome Mr. Marshall and The Executioner, the two films he really adored making and that he felt were his best successes abroad. Although his post at the Filmoteca Nacional is honorary, Berlanga believes himself to be one of the few Spanish filmmakers who is truly an "archeologist of the cinema": he would like to discover a film print technique that would never wear away. Currently, he is involved in a program for the preservation of all Spanish films but complains that the present government does not give him financial backing. Even the Reagan administration used to provide funds for the preservation of Spanish films, but severe economic cutbacks in the United States have precipitated an end to a program for restoring selected Spanish films. [5]

Continuing our discussion at his chalet in Somosaguas (a suburb of Madrid), Berlanga introduced me to his wife and four sons, one of whom is presently working in the film industry. Berlanga told me he has always found it easy to direct actors, from early on in his career to the present. He always looks for natural actors--in fact the Marquis in Patrimonio nacional was a real one and had never acted before in his lifetime. I asked him to single out his best films and he chose three, all of which will be discussed in ensuing paragraphs because they most aptly sum up Berlanga's entire oeuvre. These are Bienvenido Sr. Marshall (1952), El verdugo (1963) and Escopeta nacional (1978). [6] These films demonstrate how Berlanga began his career as a neo-realist imitator with "picaresque" tendencies, moved into social satire tinged with black humor, giving his films an international dimension, and finally, created his own hermetic yet financially profitable "personal" cinema, a style which continues to please him and his public into the 1980s.

Welcome Mr. Marshall won honorable mention at the Cannes Film Festival in 1953. A gentle, humorous satire about the local village reaction to Marshall Plan aid, it is set in the small Castilian town of Villar del Río, a local village which has the usual quiet church, serene plaza and simple people you would find in any Southern Spanish town. A surprise visit from the governor disturbs the town's customary tranquillity as all the farmers rush off to hide their harvest produce, fearing the governor has come to take stock of it. The latter, however, has come to tell of the impending visit of the Marshall Plan Commission to Villar del Río. The entire village must get ready to meet the Commission because the amount of monetary aid given will depend upon what the

Two scenes from <u>Welcome Mr. Marshall</u>, directed by Luis G. Berlanga (1953).

official delegation views as necessary in each town and what "kindnesses" these Americans receive from the local farmers. Nevertheless, the townspeople cannot foresee what actually happens. Their Mayor, played by José Isbert, together with an impresario (Manolo Moran), organizes a special folkloric reception, an Andalusian fiesta setting--women with shawls, mantillas and castanets, bullfighters, all designed to seduce Mr. Marshall. The villagers invest all their pesetas in creating this stereotype, dream-like vision of a town in Southern Spain, masking their own misery and poverty, dreaming of future wealth and riches because of Mr. Marshall. Their dreams are soon shattered when the official convoy sweeps through town in three autos that do not stop for an instant, leaving the townspeople in a great cloud of dust. They are desolate and all their hopes and dreams of future wealth vanish. The film, however, abounds in flashes of malicious humor, and finely observed satirical touches concerning the United States. In two dream sequences, Berlanga presents the villagers' view of the American Old West, replete with saloon, gambling wheels, gunfights and bar girls; his other images of the Ku Klux Klan and the House Committee on Un-American Activities-McCarthy Hearings are also adroitly portrayed. When the film was first shown in Cannes, Edward G. Robinson (an American actor) denounced the film for its anti-American bias and managed to have it censored. During these years of the Cold War, the film was obviously misunderstood. Rather than an anti-American satire, it was a burlesque of a small village eager to disfigure itself in order to get the promised benefits of Marshall Plan aid.

Although Plácido was nominated for an Academy Award in 1961 in the Best Foreign Film Category, Berlanga believes his real talent is as a satirist in the great Spanish picaresque tradition, and that this was exemplified more fully and maturely in El verdugo. In Plácido, "I wanted to show only the goodness of men through the social order of mankind. As a man, I am a liberal, as an individual, a Christian. What pleases me is to make films. I like to live and be left in peace."[8] Plácido dealt with the collective loneliness of thirty men lost in Burgos during a Christian charity campaign. "They carry out a kind of strange, infernal and pointless pilgrimage ... which Berlanga transforms into a feverish enquiry into the absurd,"[9] that is, into the vanity and frustrations of Spanish society.

El verdugo (The Executioner, 1963) is, for me, Berlanga's finest film. It is always chosen, along with Welcome Mr. Marshall, as one of the best ten films ever to come out of Spain. A bitter black comedy about a reluctant hangman, it won prizes in Venice, Cannes and Moscow. Scripted by Rafael Azcona and Berlanga himself, El verdugo tells the story of José Luis (masterfully played by the Italian actor Nino Manfredi), an undertaker's assistant who wishes to marry the daughter of the local hangman. He agrees to become her father's apprentice and successor in order to qualify for the municipal apartment that goes along with the job. Besides, prisoners are usually pardoned in Spain before they are to be garroted. Forced to marry because of the hangman's daughter's pregnancy, Manfredi begins to enjoy life until his father-in-law unexpectedly retires and Manfredi becomes the hangman. Here the film turns to real drama as he is dragged in at one point to perform his duty on a calm and dignified political prisoner. Berlanga attacks the custom of garroting and capital punishment in Spain, and as a result the film was severely cut by the Spanish censors. El verdugo is bitter, yet highly amusing, "a curious blending of the merry and the macabre ... a frothy domestic farce on the surface, it is actually a bitter indictment of capital punishment."[10] Transcending his neo-realist style, Berlanga is at his best because he uses his morbid sense of humor to crystallize, comment upon and perhaps change one of the most ghastly punishments in Spanish society.

Berlanga had indeed progressed from a gentle satirist of the 1950s to a mordant one of the late 1960s. His latest films, of the 1970s and '80s, however, no longer possess the spirit of biting satire and mordant anarchy as in his earlier films. During the earlier decades his satirical view of Spanish reality boldly and successfully blended sarcasm, allegory and hyperbole. His latest films display a mercurial temperament and a taste for coarse and sometimes scatological humor which has crystallized into a sardonic and grim view of human nature.

National Shotgun (1978) and National Trust (1980) are Berlanga's most commercially popular films to date and the first ones to take advantage of the newly gained freedom of

---

Opposite: at top, José Luis López Vásquez in Placido (1961); below, Nino Manfredi (with suitcase) in El verdugo (The Hangman or Not on Your Life) (1963).

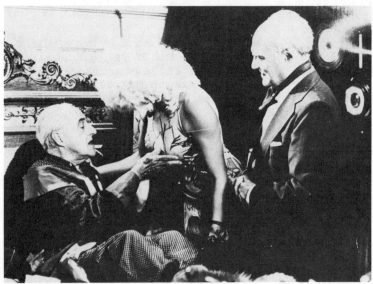

Above and opposite, three scenes from Berlanga's National Shotgun (1978). At top on opposite page, Luis Escobar and Elsa Zabda. Above, José Luis López Vásquez.

expression since Franco's death. These films are extremely
personal ones, peculiarly Spanish and too difficult to sub-
title into English. Catalán and other dialects are spoken
throughout by the actors and Berlanga felt that National Trust
was not "international enough in appeal."[11] The French
critics at Cannes in 1981 savaged the film, and its director.
Even Andrew Sarris, the esteemed film critic of the Village
Voice, agreed with the French, characterizing National Trust
as a "talkathon of actors as if directed by Max Ophuls and
several others,"[12] and implying a new "eclecticism" in Berlanga's style.[13]

Shotgun and Trust are very humorous films. Both
were shot on location in and outside of Madrid. Thematically,
they deal with a group of self-exiled aristocrats who return
to Madrid. Shotgun, a satire of questionable taste on ad-
ministrators and investments, is set in Catalonia on a huge
hunting estate. To sum up its plot briefly, a Catalonian
gentleman has been advised to promote his business interests
by getting to know the "right" people. With this in mind, he
organizes a costly hunting party on the estate of an old Marquis named Leguineche. The "right" people turn out to be a
disastrous group of rabble, decadents, crooks, freeloaders,
sexual deviants and movie stars. The party begins badly and
becomes worse. The Marquis' middle-aged delinquent and
perverted son (admirably portrayed by José Luis López
Vásquez) kidnaps the Prime Minister's movie star mistress.
The old Marquis complains of the rudeness of these guests
who are filled with bitchiness. The film concludes in an
orgy of frustrated and satiated sexual appetites, voyeurism
and chronic indigestion. Just as the Catalonian is on the
verge of obtaining the Minister's ear, there is a reshuffling
of the cabinet and all his political and sexual efforts go for
naught.

Trust is a worthy successor, enumerating the problems
encountered by aristocrats when they return from self-
imposed exile. A multitude of themes abound: the clash
between rustic and urban society, epitomized by their problems
in using automobiles instead of farm animals; the new freedom in sexuality and the use of hair transplants are also
discussed. The "plot" is an excuse for Berlanga to comment
upon a variety of themes. During the transition from country
to city life, the Marquesa falls ill and dies. Her husband
turns their palace into a museum in order to pay the bills
and taxes. Berlanga used an old palace near the Plaza de
Cíbeles in Madrid where the government let him film freely.

In fact, the city of Madrid was never photographed so beautifully as in both these color films. Trust carries the same
personages and themes forward in time to the first few years
of the reign of Juan Carlos, when the Marquesa tries to revive the pomp of traditional court life in her palace in
Madrid.

A second sequel, Nacional Tres, opened just after
Christmas in 1983 but has not yet been seen in the United
States. Yet another moral tale about the hazards of oppor-
tunism and the deception of patrons, it is done in the form
of a popular farce--rude, jolly and often vulgar, but funny.
Berlanga has reworked the same theme three successive
times to satirize the aristocratic decay and the political
chicanery of the Spaniards.

Amparo Soler Leal and José Luis López Vásquez in Nacional
Tres (1982).

Some critics feel that Shotgun, Trust and National
Three are all good examples of the "new Spanish cinema"
since Berlanga, "with a light, farcical touch mocks the side
show of the powers that have ruled the country--priests,
venal politicans, aristocrats, prostitutes, businessmen."[14]
The films will mean more to Spaniards than to other national

groups because the sense of humor and satire and the target stereotypes are essentially Spanish. Though some of the antics among the films' characters border on the grotesqueness of opera buffa, Berlanga has given them spicy dialogue and enough humor and wit to maintain our interest. The trilogy represents the newest type of exposé of Spanish manners and morals by an old master satirist. Vulgarity has replaced subtle humor and sensitivity. "Berlanga has shrewdly observed a Spanish microcosm of life--reckless politicians, lewd aristocrats, ultramundane clergymen and giggly starlets in a disintegrating world where corruption and incompetence predominate."[15]

It is clear that Berlanga has changed his narrative point of view over the last thirty years. Beginning as a traditionalist filmmaker, imitating the Italian neo-realist school, he developed his own brand of social realism in the Fifties and Sixties, keeping his characters and plots scaled down. With the advent of the New Wave of Spanish Cinema since Franco's death, his films have grown more operatic. Many more personnages populate his frames and, sacrificing intimacy, Berlanga utilizes a new, highly sophisticated technique of deep-focus and planned sequence shooting. Berlanga has replaced intimacy with a provocative use of actors densely populating the frame while using a peculiar long-shot syntax, evolving a new and highly original style, which we might perhaps call the "choral" type of film. Although Berlanga is now enjoying his long sought-after success at age 64, I feel he is no longer looking for Spanish subjects that are larger than life, that bypass Spain's national borders. He will always reflect his critical, anarchic, revisionist spirit in whatever screenplay he chooses to write or film. But the years have mellowed him and although he has achieved commercial success, his last three films in the 1980s are a prolongation of one enormously funny joke which is fast losing our interest. His eye for satire remains acute, but his style is overbearing and repetitious; his dialogues obfuscate the narrative which is becoming more clouded as the years go by. Although Berlanga may now be substituting commercial values for acute, intimate perceptions, he has left an indelible imprint on all of modern Spanish cinema.

Bibliography

Hernández-Les & Hidalgo. El último austro-húngaro: Conversaciones con Berlanga. Barcelona: Ed. Anagrama, 1981.

Articles

Berlanga, Luis G. "The Day I Refused to Work." Films & Filming (Dec. 1961), 9-10, 40.

Besa, Peter. "Review of National Shotgun." Variety (May 10, 1978), 27.

Besa, Peter. "Review of Patrimonio nacional." Variety (Apr. 29, 1981), 18.

Besa, Peter. "Review of Nacional Tres." Variety (Apr. 25, 1984), 22.

Cobos, Juan. "Spanish Fighter." Films & Filming (Feb. 1958), 12.

Crowther, B. "Review of El verdugo." New York Times (May 30, 1965), 52.

Galán, Diego. Carta abierta a Berlanga. (Huelva: Semana de cine ibero-americano, 1978), 54 pages.

Marías, Miguel. "El patrimonio de Berlanga." Casablanca (Apr. 1981), 23-29.

Mosk. "Review of Welcome Mr. Marshall." Variety (July 29, 1953), 18.

Zunzunegui, Santos. "Review of National Trust." Contra-campo (Jun-July, 1981), 62-63.

Monographs

Dirigido por (May 1974), 1-24. Entire issue devoted to Berlanga.

Berlanga, Luis. Entire monograph devoted to Berlanga, published by the Filmoteca Nacional, Ed. Victoria, 1982, 78 pages.

Chapter 5

JOSE LUIS BORAU (1929)

Filmography

Short films: 1962--Capital: Madrid; 1963--Bellezas de Mallorca.

Features: 1963--Brandy; 1964--Crimen de doble filo; 1973--Hay que matar a B (B Must Die); 1974--Furtivos (Poachers); 1979--La Sabina (The Sabina); 1983-84--Río abajo (On the Line).

José Luis Borau was born in Zaragoza on August 8, 1929 and received a Law degree in 1954 from the University there. He also worked as a film critic for the Aragon Herald and other newspapers and magazines until 1956. He moved to Madrid where he joined the National Film School and received his diploma in 1961, directing his first short subject, La despedida (The Farewell), and afterwards, En el río (On the River). He has been concerned with many aspects of film including teaching courses in direction. In fact, in 1965, he returned to I. I. E. C. and took up a professorship in screenwriting.

Borau always considered himself a student of American cinema. His first feature film, Brandy, the Sheriff of Lokatumba, starred American actor Alex Nicol and was one of the few Spanish westerns made in Spain in the early 1960s before the eruption of the Italian "spaghetti-western" phenomenon. His second film, Crimen de doble filo (Double-edged Murder) is a psychological thriller stylistically in the manner of the great Hollywood films noirs of Lang or Hitchcock, but set entirely in Madrid. In 1967, Borau also began to film TV commercials and founded his own production company, El Imán, S.A., which produced Jaime de Armiñán's My

José Luis Borau

Dearest Señorita (1973) (see Chapter 1) and Camada negra (Black Brood) directed by Manolo Gutiérrez Aragón (see Chapter 13).

Together with another successful film producer, Luis Megino, Borau directed his third film, a political thriller with an international cast, Hay que matar a B (B Must Die) in 1973. It starred Darren McGavin, Patricia Neal, Stephane Audran and Burgess Meredith and has been shown in the United States on American television. B Must Die, a Spanish-Swiss co-production was made in an original English version as well as a Spanish one and, according to Borau himself, "It was probably one of the most sophisticated and corrosive films ever made in Spain dealing with assassination."[1] It won several awards. However, Borau's international reputation was truly established by his next two films: Furtivos (Poachers), which is very well known in England and the United States, treating "life in a symbolical forest where freedom is an appearance,"[2] and La Sabina (The Sabina) (1979), a Spanish co-production portraying "the story of modern man and the mysteries of nature and ancient legends, notably a mythical dragon who makes love to men and then devours them."[3]

Borau finds every film he makes a challenge.[4] In fact, he has been occupied with a project tentatively titled Río abajo (On the Line), with a script by Barbra Probst Solomon. Currently being shot in Laredo and San Antonio, Texas, the original cast included Julie Carmen, Tommy Lee Jones or Dennis Hopper and Michael O'Keefe.[5] Expected for release in 1984 on American screens, Río abajo now stars David Carradine, Victoria Abril, Scott Wilson and Jeff Delger. Borau told me about his difficulties in filming in the United States, with unions, script writers, budgets, etc., but he has always been eager and felt the need to make films outside of Spain. In fact, Borau is probably the most cosmopolitan and international of all the Spanish film-makers I have met. With the exception of Furtivos, all his feature films contain resonances of the best directors of European cinema, especially Fritz Lang. Borau indicated that film is his only consuming passion. (He has been close to marriage many times but still remains a bachelor.)[6] Besides his new project, currently filming in Texas, and a biography he is writing on silent film star and director Henri d'Arrast, Borau divides his time between homes he owns in Madrid and Sherman Oaks, California and continues to direct and produce films for his own production company, El Imán.

Borau's best films are all tightly scripted stories, realistic screenplays which contain sharp and startling images (he admits that Carl Dreyer and Fritz Lang influenced him greatly.)[7] Early Borau films are stylistically eclectic--viz. the film noir influences in Double-edged Murder and B Must Die. But it was Poachers, his most "Spanish" film with all of its peculiar naturalistic features firmly rooted in the Spanish tradition, that has made Borau an international celebrity. Borau himself cannot explain the success of Poachers.[8] A brief analysis of his best films may give some clues to the direction and shape of his future career here and abroad.

Crimen de doble filo (Double-edged Crime) is an interesting film that pays homage to Alfred Hitchcock. The plot is terse: a young male resident of an apartment building runs into the cellar of his building and finds the janitor dead. He spies a man running out of the cellar wearing a white coat, and believes him to be the murderer. The man in the white coat turns out to be his own wife's American lover who wants her to reveal their affair to her husband. The husband shoots his wife's lover because he fears that the American believes he has killed the janitor. However, we learn in a subsequent flashback that it was the wife who killed the janitor. She had been molested by him and received constant threatening phone calls from him. Tolerating no more, she hits the janitor on the head with a heavy candle and leaves him to die. Both husband and wife are arrested for different murders and pass each other in the hallway of the local police station, realizing that their lives have been totally destroyed by deception and adultery. Crimen is a tightly scripted, small thriller film in the mode of noir with a surprising denouement. It could have been dubbed into any language and made anywhere in the world, which indicates Borau's propensity for an "international" cinema and "international" marketing of films. Because Crimen starred two Spanish actors unknown to international audiences, Carlos Estrada and Susana Campos, however, the film has hardly ever been shown outside of Spain.

B Must Die continues Borau's desire to reach international audiences. He gathered four bankable actors together for this Spanish-Swiss co-production, Darren McGavin, Patricia Neal, Stephane Audran and Burgess Meredith. Co-scripted by film director and scenarist Antonio Drove, B Must Die is the story of a loser, McGavin, whose partner is killed in a trucking accident somewhere in Latin America where the truckers are on strike. McGavin wants to earn enough money to return to his native Hungary and begins to look

Patricia Neal in Borau's B Must Die (1973). Opposite, in
scenes from the same film, Stephane Audran and Darren
McGavin (top), and Burgess Meredith and McGavin.

money to return to his native Hungary and begins to look
for another job. He is set up by Burgess Meredith (a local
police agent in plain clothes) with money to woo a French
woman (Audran) who is the mistress of a beer magnate named
Daniels. The latter is found dead in Audran's apartment
and the police theorize that McGavin killed him in a jealous
rage over the woman. This sub-plot is a ruse, since the
police swap McGavin's innocent plea for a murder they want
him to commit: a man named B will step off an Iberian jet-
liner and McGavin will be released after he kills B with a
high-powered rifle armed with telescopic lenses. McGavin
does the job and is machine-gunned down in turn by local
police. Patricia Neal gives a credible supporting performance
as McGavin's long-suffering mistress. She recognizes
McGavin's need for a better life but realizes he is a loser.

Borau was forced by the Spanish censors to re-locate
the action to an un-specified Latin American country instead
of the original Basque locale where the script was shot. B
Must Die echoes many Fritz Lang films where the protagonist
is "an outcast manipulated by powerful and secret machinery."[9]
The moving story of fading love between McGavin and Neal
provides a good counterpoint to the film's central plot.

Borau has shown a penchant for writing and directing classy genre films which demonstrate his deep admiration for the "classic" Hollywood directors. When Poachers was released in 1976-77, therefore, it was a totally unexpected effort from Borau. Lacking "international perspectives" and "Hollywood influences," Poachers is still Borau's best film of his career and, critically, his most "Spanish" product.

Poachers is the story of Angel and his mother Martina who live in the forests around Segovia and earn their living by hunting wild game and selling the meat and skins for profit. Because trapping has been outlawed, Angel must resort to furtive deception of the local civil guards in order to survive while living off the forest. Martina's foster-son, her favorite, is the local governor of the province (played brilliantly by the director), who comes to hunt and visit his foster-mother. One day Angel, played by Ovidi Montllor, goes to the provincial capital to buy traps, rope and nooses and meets an under-age girl, Milagros (played by Alicia Sánchez), who is the mistress of a well-known delinquent, El Cuqui. Milagros has escaped from the local girl's reformatory and immediately takes up with Angel, thinking him a fool. Angel returns to the forest with her, much to the disfavor of his mother (played by Lola Gaos). Milagros plans to leave Angel and hide out from the authorities until El Cuqui comes to reclaim her. The governor, however, intervenes and Angel decides to marry the wayward girl. Happiness is brief, since El Cuqui returns and Milagros, although now fond of Angel, still plans to run off. Meanwhile, the local police discover El Cuqui's presence in the forest and Angel is hired to track him down. He pursues him and finds him, but lets him go because Milagros has promised to stay with him if her lover is spared from jail. Cuqui escapes, and Martina, Angel's mother, tells him that Milagros has fled, taking some of the family's possessions with her. Angel prospers and becomes a Forest Guard under the influence of the governor. But he is obsessed by Milagro's disappearance. He finally realizes that Martina, out of jealousy, has killed his wife. Martina takes communion at her last confession and on the way home from the Sunday church services, Angel shoots her in a field of snow.

Furtivos is one of the most brutal films ever made in Spain, portraying an oedipal relationship and its dire consequences. Lola Gaos as Martina gives the performance of her life as the mother who cannot accept losing her son to another woman. The film was made in 1975 just before

Alicia Sánchez as Milagros in Borau's <u>Furtivos</u> (<u>Poachers</u>), 1974).

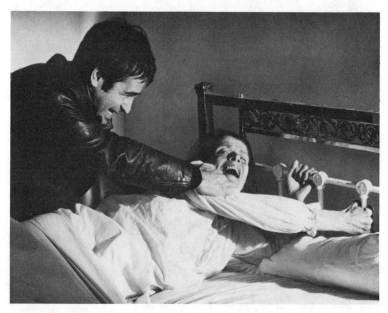

Lola Gaos as Martina (above) and with Ovidi Montllor (below) in scenes from Furtivos.

Ovidi Montllor and Alicia Sánchez in scenes from <u>Furtivos</u>--
the <u>new</u> eroticism.

Franco's death, and Borau was forced to censor certain
scenes of nudity, although there are still passages of unexpected eroticism and nudity that the censors permitted to
remain, as well as some brutal hunting scenes. Furtivos
has a double meaning in Spanish: persons hunting game
illegally (poaching) and persons who harbor secret thoughts. [10]
As a film, Furtivos is severely critical of the brutality,
physical and mental, of the Spaniard. After much hostility,
Borau finally won the battle with the Film Ministry to show
Furtivos at Cannes and abroad with no cuts. Although it was
banned in Spain, Furtivos was the sensation of the Cannes
and Berlin Film Festivals of 1976 and has been widely shown
throughout North America under the auspices of the American
Film Institute. Shot in Segovia, it cost Borau some two-
hundred thousand dollars to make; it was filmed in color and
the exteriors in the forest were very difficult to film because
of changeable weather conditions. Furtivos became the top-
grossing film in Spain in 1976 after censorship objections were
overcome, netting some three million dollars. Borau deserves his success; he had the courage to reveal, overtly,
the dark-side of the Spanish character. Although the film
begins with the statement "Spain is a peaceful forest,"
Borau demonstrates the exact opposite and clearly drama-
tizes the rebelliousness and oppression of the Spanish people
under the Franco regime. [11] Borau's battles with the Spanish
censors paved the way for many other Spanish directors to
deal with controversial themes without fear of censorship.
"The uncompromising Borau won this artistic freedom for
his colleagues ... it will be interesting to see what other
Spanish directors ... will do in exercising these new privileges." [12]

Furtivos is a stark drama with powerful sexual undertones in which primitive passion and emotion are the rule.
Borau clearly built on his past directorial experiences to
mold this terse and suspenseful drama into a mordant critique of Franco's political and religious repression which continued to impoverish the spiritual and psychological life of
the Spanish people. Furtivos is not an oblique assault on
present-day Spain but a well-told tale, excellently plotted,
containing much development of character, and set against
thrilling rustic backgrounds, which directly seeks govern-
mental reforms and paves the way to new freedoms for
Spanish filmmakers.

Retreating to the security of a big Hollywood production
(Furtivos had no bankable stars), Borau next found himself in

Andalusia, working in color and Cinemascope, with five internationally known actors, Jon Finch, Angela Molina, Harriet
Andersson, Simon Ward and Carol Kane. In spite of this
"international" cast, Andalusia itself is the star of the film
as photographed by Lars-Goram Bjorne. Bjorne is not an
expressionist photographer--the sun is the sun, night is night,
the land is the land. Realizing the need to make films that
would sell abroad, given the state of the Spanish film industry
in the late 1970s,[12] Borau obtained 30 per cent of the film's
nearly 70 million-peseta budget (nearly three-quarters of a
million dollars) from the Svensk Film Institute.

La Sabina is a very Renoir-like film and technically
different from what Borau himself calls the Fritz Lang style
of B Must Die and the naturalism of Poachers.[13] The film's
characters are firmly rooted in the Andalusian landscape
where the story takes place. The Sabina deals with three
women and two men and their strange involvement with each
other. The main character is Michael (Jon Finch), a writer
who is tracing the mystery of the disappearance of an English
writer some one hundred years before. Michael lives with
Daisy (Carol Kane) but is attracted to a village girl, Pepa
(Angela Molina), who lives with her retarded brother Manolin
(Ovidi Montllor). Pepa tells Michael about the Sabina, the
mythical dragon who lives in a cave, makes love to men and
then devours them. Michael's ex-wife Monica (Harriet Andersson arrives on the scene with her new lover, Philip (Simon
Ward), and both try to persuade Michael to return to London
and give up the mystery of the Sabina. But Michael is on
the verge of solving the mystery. He challenges Phillip to
enter the cave, and burns their lifeline with his lighter.
Michael and Philip drown in the cave's dark waters as the
group of townspeople hear sighs, whispers and explosions
within as they gather, waiting for a solution to the mystery
of the Sabina.

The Sabina is undoubtedly an important transitional
step in Borau's filmmaking career. It is a very sexual
and disturbing film, in which all the characters' actions
have very complex motivations. Michael, the writer, is
doomed from the beginning of the film, since we are aware
that the Sabina, the mythological demon-devourer of men,
will probably claim her male victim or victims at the conclusion. Michael is at a dead end anyway--his life with
Daisy is meaningless; his infatuation with Pepa will lead him
nowhere; his ex-wife lures him sexually to expose his suicidal
tendencies. Philip is the only redeeming character in the

Top, J. L. Borau rehearsing a scene with Angelina Molina
and Carol Kane; below, Harriet Andersson, Molina and Kane
in La Sabina (1979).

Entrance to the cave where Sabina dwells in Borau's La Sabina.

screenplay who does not deserve his fate. Borau makes use of the Andalusian countryside to fine effect and the colors of Ronda and other small Andalusian towns are startingly crisp and real. Borau has also successfully revived the mysterious myth and romanticism of the Andalusian woman to fine effect, preferring to emphasize in his story the jaded intellectual's ephemeral love and fatalism that completely engulf him and lead him to tragic consequences. Borau had planned this film so that his characters moved freely in the Andalusian landscape: "In the whole film, there are only two close-ups."[13] English critic Roger Mortimore considers La Sabina "a resolutely unfashionable film."[14] Borau's courage, even recklessness, one hopes, will pay off at the box office.

David Carradine, Jeff Delger and Victoria Abril in Borau's Río Abajo (On the Line, 1983).

José Luis Borau is a very gutsy actor, producer, and director. He is a solid talent who faces new challenges, takes chances. He is a formidable opponent of censorship and, like St. Paul, always seeks some new thing. His experience in filming Río abajo in the United States may well strengthen his career and give him the international recognition he so richly deserves.[15] Borau is perhaps the best propagandist for Spanish cinema, his fellow film directors, and the National Film School, in and outside of Spain.   His personal and professional efforts on behalf of the Spanish film industry will surely be recognized in the years ahead.

Bibliography

Besa, Peter.   "Review of Furtivos. "   Variety (June 18, 1975), 18.

Besa, Peter.   "Review of La Sabina. "   Variety (Dec. 26, 1979), 12.

Besa, Peter.   "Borau's Latest, On the Line, A Problematic 4-Year Odyssey. " Variety (July 11, 1984), 35.

Besa, Peter.   "Review of Río abajo (On the Line), " Variety (Dec. 19, 1984), 19, 88.

Crist, Judith.   "Review of Furtivos. "   New York Post (Mar. 7, 1978), 42.

Heredero, Carlos F.   "J. L. Borau: La belleza y la racional- idad de un clásico. " Argumentos (Feb. 1980), 47-51.

Hernández-Les, J.   "Review of La Sabina. "   Cinema 2002 (Dec. 1959), 19.

Maslin, Janet.   "Review of Furtivos. "   New York Times (Mar. 7, 1978), 44.

Mortimore, Roger.   "Reporting from Madrid. "   Sight & Sound (Summer 1980), 156-158, 188.

"Review of Crimen de doble filo. "   Film IDEAL (Oct. 1965), 716.

"Interview with J. L. Borau. "   Dirigido por (Jul-Aug. 1975), 34-40.

"Entretien avec J. L. Borau. "   Image et son (Sept. 1977), 76-82.

Chapter 6

JAIME CAMINO (1936)

Filmography

Short films: 1960--Contrastes (16 mm.); 1962--Centauros;
El toro, vida y muerte; 1965--Copa Davis.

Features: 1963--Los felices 60; 1966--Mañana será otro día;
1968--España otra vez; 1969--Jutrzenka (Un invierno en Mallorca); 1973--Mi profesor particular; 1976--Las largas vacaciones del 36 (The Long Holidays of 1936); 1977--La vieja
memoria (The Old Memory); 1980--La campanada; 1984--El
balcon abierto (The Open Balcony).

Most Spanish filmmakers begin their prolific careers
by first obtaining law degrees, then entering the National
Film School.   Jaime Camino is no exception.   Born in Barcelona on June 11, 1936, he first studied at a Jesuit college,
took his Law degree at the University of Barcelona, and
demonstrated other talents as a music teacher.   He studied
and taught piano and harmony.   He also showed talent as a
film critic, writing for Indice and Nuestro Cine in the early
1960s.   In 1961, he directed his first short in 16mm.,
Contrastes, collaborating on the script with author Manuel
Mira.   In 1962, he began using 35mm. film and directed
two more short features: Centauros and El toro, vida y
muerte.   By 1963 he was ready to begin his first feature
film, Los felices 60.

A graduate of the Institut de Cinema Català (The
Catalan Film Institute), Camino is also a talented novelist,
winning the Nadal Prize in 1960, and usually collaborates
on the scripts for his feature films.   No stranger to the
documentary, he has made several films about the Spanish
Civil War, the one event and theme which dominates his
artistry.

Jaime Camino (photo courtesy Filmoteca Nacional, Madrid)

His last book to appear in Spain on this subject was Intimas conversaciones con La Pasionara in 1977. Currently the owner of Tibidabo Films and helping continually to finance the Catalan film industry, Camino has always had a guaranteed commercial distributor. His principal subject, the Civil War, also guarantees commercial success in Spain. Camino has never had much trouble from the censors because, whether his screenplays are factual or fictional, they nearly always favor the victors of the war, the Nationalists. When The Long Holidays of 1936 was released in Spain, however, for the first time Camino portrayed the victors as evil and the losers (Communists or Reds) as good.

Most of Camino's early films, including the controversial España otra vez, with a script by Camino, Román Gubern and Alvah Bessie (one of the "Hollywood Ten"), which was nominated for the Academy Award for Best Foreign Film of 1968, are full of good intentions. Camino has great ambitions as a filmmaker, but is generally unsuccessful at realizing them because most of his films are either poorly scripted and edited or lack the vigor to sustain their thematic promise even if carefully and professionally photographed and edited. This was true, at least, until Camino made The Long Holidays of 1936.

Most critics would agree that Camino is a careful and professional filmmaker. All his color films are especially well photographed and contain images of strength, beauty and subtlety. However, they falter dramatically: the characters have little motivation and much of the dialogue seems static. Camino is frequently accused of "pedestrian" direction and of choosing banal subjects. Nevertheless, when he inserts documentary footage into his "fictional" films, the screen comes alive. Too much documentary footage, however, can bore the viewer.

La vieja memoria (1977), nearly three hours in length, was a big commercial success in Spain. Its technique is fascinating: live testimony from different participants in the Spanish Civil War is intercut with newsreel footage of the war. We see La Pasionara, for example, reflect upon her triumphs as a young Communist. Other footage is devoted to the emergence of Franco and Primo de Rivera as leaders and everyone in 1976-77 who had met them is urged to reflect upon his or her role at that time. La vieja memoria is a memorable film because of the nature of its testimony and each informant's particular search for the "truth" behind these events. Camino utilized interview techniques similar to those in Marcel Ophul's monumental six-hour film, Le chagrin et la pitié (The Sorrow & the Pity) which were later taken up by American director Warren Beatty for his gigantic opus Reds, treating the life of John Reed and the Russian Revolution; Beatty, however, did not reveal the names of his informants. The frequent repetition in Camino's film and its exaggerated length diminish the viewer's interest in an otherwise extraordinary film.

Although La vieja memoria was made almost two years later than The Long Vacations of 1936, it is the earlier film that shows Camino's greatest cohesion and maturity as a filmmaker. Vacations is the story of two families in a Catalonian town caught in the throes of the Civil War. The film begins in 1936 and ends in 1939. Vacations delineates a series of relationships between men and women over this three-year period. The best "story" is that of

Opposite, documentary footage from Camino's La vieja memoria (The Old Memory, 1977)

Quique and Alicia. Quique dies in the war and Alicia mourns.
The family who supported the Reds must leave their homes
as General Franco marches into Catalonia.   There is an
interesting sub-plot about a father who refuses to fight and a
son who enlists to maintain the family's pride and courage.
Angela Molina, one of Spain's most popular actresses, plays
a maid, Encarna, who must return to her local village because her family needs her.   We witness the trials and
tribulations of the Catalonians as the children grow up and
mature amid the adversities of war.   Francisco Rabal, the
very popular Spanish actor, is surprisingly good in the small
role of the ''Red'' school teacher who is ill, starving and left
to die.   Although the film suggests many political motivations,
it is essentially not political in nature.   It is really about
how people survive during wartime, how children who began
the summer of 1936 with childish games ended playing at war
by the summer of 1939, and demonstrates how war was the
most traumatic phenomenon in their young lives.   Another
Catalan writer, José María Gironella, wrote a great Civil
War trilogy beginning with The Cypresses Believe in God
which traced the fate of the Alvear family from 1931 to 1939,

Jaime Camino (center) directing Las largas vacaciones del
36 (1976).

and Camino in this film is recreating Gironella's characters, although on a much smaller scale. "Rather than depict the war itself, Camino and his script-writers have opted for an indirect approach in which political and military situations increasingly impinge upon the life of the bourgeois family."[1]

There are no real central characters in the film (everyone is important, whether aristocrat or peasant) and Camino's anti-Franco sympathies are daringly evident; his pro-Franco characters are all depicted as bumbling and superficial. Vacations was made during the very last days before Franco's death and given this timing, is surprisingly frank.

The film's best scenes are those which show the atmosphere of the Catalan family and the continuance of its life style through all the disruption created by the war. The film is richly textured and features a grand cast of well-known popular Spanish actors, among them the very beautiful Angela Molina, Ismael Merlo, Francisco Rabal and José Sacristán. Yet, "despite its truthful insights into everyday life ... it is seriously impaired by a sentimental treatment of the child characters and gives a grossly parodic and complacent view of the Francoist figures."[2] Certainly, Vacations is not the definitive film about family life during Spain's Civil War era. It seems that Camino and his co-scenarist Manolo Gutiérrez Aragón intended to collaborate on a purely commercial work for general consumption by the Spanish public. But like most films that combine commercial appeal with intellectual premises, Camino's tend to be moderately successful in Spain. Few of them, with the exception of Vacations, are ever shown abroad. Many of Camino's films have lost their dramatic impact because of censorship restrictions.[3] With these restrictions having been lifted since 1977, it will be interesting to see what direction his career takes. When I last spoke with Camino in Madrid in 1982, he was working on a script based upon a novel entitled La bomba (The Bomb). His career is at the crossroads and his public is still waiting for a trenchant and truly aesthetically satisfying film work from one of Spain's youngest Catalonian directors.

Bibliography

Besa, Peter. "Review of La campanada (Leaving It All)." Variety (Apr. 16, 1980), p. 28.

Besa, Peter. "Review of El balcon abierto." Variety (Sept. 4, 1984), 18.

Davis, Russell. "Review of Las largas vacaciones del 36." London Observer (Oct. 30, 1977), 43.

Riambau, Esteve. "Review of La vieja memoria." Dirigido por No. 58 (1972), 49.

"Interview with Jaime Camino." Contracampo (Apr. 1979), 16-20.

"Interview with Jaime Camino." Dirigido por (May 1980), 48-53.

Chapter 7

FERNANDO COLOMO (1946)

Filmography

Short films: 1964--Sssoufl (8 mm.); 1965--Vampiro, S.A.; 1972--Mañana llega el presidente; 1975--En un París imaginario; 1976--Vd. va a ser mamá, Pomporrutas imperiales; Konensünatten (sketch for Cuentos eróticos).

Feature films: 1977--Tigres de papel; 1978--¿Qué hace una chica como tú en un sitio como éste?; 1980--La mano negra (The Black Hand); 1982--Estoy en crísis (I'm in Crisis); 1983--La línea del cielo (Skyline).

       Fernando Colomo is one of the youngest film directors currently working in Spain or abroad. Born in Madrid in 1946, he became interested in films at a very early age as a boy and started to make his own shorts at age sixteen. Also a serious painter, Colomo preferred to turn to architecture and design. His interest in films, however, persisted strongly and he entered the National Film School in Madrid in 1971. With money earned as an architect, he financed his first 16mm. short, Mañana llega el presidente, about the arrival of Argentina's former President Cámpora in Spain. The short was needlessly censored by the Franco regime. In 1975, Colomo turned out another short feature entitled En un París imaginario; it won first prize at the International Short Films Festival in Huesca (Spain) and was named the best short film of the year by the magazine Reseña. Colomo scripted and directed two other short films in 1976: Vd. va a ser mamá and Pomporrutas imperiales, which won prizes in Huesca and Madrid. Colomo also wrote several scripts for films directed by other Spaniards but made his own directorial debut in 1977 with Tigres de papel (Paper Tigers).

Fernando Colomo (left) on a set with Luis García Berlanga.

Tigers is the story of a young divorced couple. Carmen and Juan, and their relationship with their son Ivan while they remain separated. Another couple, Alberto and Carmen, who met on a holiday trip in Italy, become entwined in the progressing relationship of the separated parents. Because the film demonstrated a certain youthful spontaneity and the story appeared to reflect accurately the lives of the young modern married couples of contemporary Madrid, Colomo received plaudits from the Spanish film critics.

His second film, ¿Qué hace una chica como tú en un sitio como éste? (What's a Girl Like You Doin' in a Place Like This?), is a companion piece to Tigres. Once again, it treats the problems of modern young couples living in Madrid, married, separated, and with children who add to the problems of the adults. The performances of Hector Alterio, Carmen Maura and Felix Rotatacta are superior to those of the actors in Tigres de papel, and the film demonstrates a new candor, revealing with franchise the sexual couplings possible in the world of Rock and Pop which was just beginning to take hold upon Madrid society in the late Seventies.

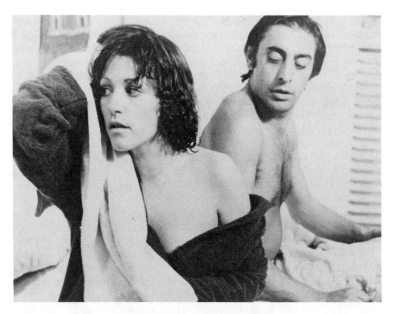

Above, Concha Gregori and Pedro D. del Corral in Colomo's Tigres de papel (Paper Tigers, 1977); below, Virginia Mataix and Iñigo Gurrea in La mano negra (The Black Hand, 1980)-- photo courtesy of Whit Stillman International.

Colomo's third film, La mano negra (The Black Hand),
filmed in 1980, begins to show the director's talent for quick
dialogue.   Filmed as a spoof of the mystery or detective
genre, Black Hand deals with an unmarried 33-year-old man,
living at home with his parents.   One day, he meets an old
school chum, a writer of mystery novels.   In their youth
they used to belong to a group called "La mano negra."   For
some unexplained reason, a "third" man wants to kill the
mystery writer and after nearly an hour of dialogue, romance
and some nudity, the film moves into an exciting conclusive
scene in which the star, Iñigo Gurrea, pulls on the hand of
a statue in an isolated apartment, which causes his potential
"killer" to be electrocuted.   The writer and the "hero" then
flee the scene in a waiting helicopter.

Colomo mentions the word "macguffin" in the script,
an obvious homage to Alfred Hitchcock.   In La mano negra,
though, Colomo may be using a Hitchcock ploy in his screenplay, but there is no real irony or meaning in the use of
the ruse in the film, and it did not please this author or any
of the Spanish film critics.   Called a "comedy," La mano
negra does contain many interesting dialogue scenes but its
plot is both confusing and confused.   The film lacks continuity and is aimed at a limited youth-oriented public.   It is
well acted but the scenes of nudity and sexuality are gratuitous,
as if Colomo were really testing the new reforms in government censorship.   La mano negra has its charms as purely
escapist cinema; it is an interesting but unartistic endeavor.

Colomo's best and most aesthetically pleasing film to
date is Estoy en crísis (I'm in a Crisis, 1982) which was
Spain's 1982 entry to the Venice Film Fesitval.   Starring
the popular actor José Sacristán, Crisis was shot in Madrid
and Segovia.   It is the story of an advertising executive,
Bernabé, who is bored with his job, his wife and two daughters
and is presently trying to seduce any young woman who comes
his way.   While filming a TV commercial for the honey industry, he meets a seventeen-year-old model, Lucía, a hippie-
type, very 1980s.   She smokes pot, believes in living in a
commune, eats health foods, etc.   As counterpoint to this
relationship, Sacristán also seduces a young advertising
executive who is on the way to the top and who, incidentally,
has better and more promising ideas than he has about marketing for "females."   Continually making a fool of himself
with the hippies, Bernabé decides to leave his wife, Gloria,
and with his hippie model and the entire commune, sets out
for a friend's estate in Segovia.   Taking the young hippie

Scene from Colomo's Estoy en crísis (I'm in a Crisis, 1982), with José Sacristán and unidentified actress. Below, poster art advertising the film.

model to bed, Sacristán is alarmed when she refuses him--
a put down of the old Spanish machísmo.

Several days later, the owner of the estate, Sebastián,
becomes aware of the break-up between Bernabé and Gloria
and proposes to Gloria that they live together. Unable to
tolerate her hypocritical marriage to Bernabé, Gloria agrees.
Bernabé hears about his wife's new amorous liaison and
asserts his marital rights, but to little effect. Bernabé has
become disenchanted with "communal" life and the younger
generation. He finds himself completely alone, unable to
admit his errors of judgment and counting his losses. At
the conclusion, we see his ex-wife Gloria and her new lover,
Benavides, locked in battle like conjugal mates even though
they are not married. Bernabé sums up his agony at one
point: "I'm going into my forties and I don't understand
what's happening; I don't like my work; my wife doesn't
understand me; my family oppresses me; I'm in a crisis."[1]

Crisis is Colomo's best film. It has a universal theme
(masculine menopause) and one can compare it to the American
(Texas) film on the same theme, Middle-age Crazy, which
starred Bruce Dern and Ann-Margret. Crisis benefits from
a tight script, a catchy title song and a trenchant critique of
Spanish machísmo, marriage, the hippie generation and,
above all, capitalism which tends to dehumanize life and
subordinate the natural values of mankind to the mechanical.
Illustrating this point, there is one scene near the conclusion
where a hippie pours sand into the gas tanks of bulldozers
which threaten to invade and destroy the natural landscape
and beauty of Segovia, ripping up land, tearing down trees
for the sake of building a modern swimming pool. Crisis
is full of richly observed details about contemporary
Madrillians and their marriages.

Colomo represents a new breed of filmmaker in
Spain. He is young, married, and going through many of
the experiences his characters portray in his early films.
He is very much anti-Establishment, like Borau and Berlanga, his former professors. Like the newer generation
of filmmakers, he prefers to associate with younger artists
like Fernando Trueba, Alfonso Bermejo and others who are
cornering the "youth" audience in Spain.

When I last spoke to Colomo, he was filming in New
York in the summer of 1983, living in a rented apartment
on West 9th Street in Greenwich Village, shooting another

Antonio Resines, in dark glasses, and Colomo, checking the sound, on location with <u>Skyline</u> (1983). Photo courtesy of Stillman International.

of those "youth-oriented" films for Spanish audiences. He
was also working on a script tentatively titled El mono loco
(The Crazy Monkey.)[2]

Colomo's latest film, La línea de cielo (Skyline, 1983)
was presented in New York in April 1984 as part of the
Museum of Modern Art's New Directors/New Films Series.
It was the hit of the festival. Although Colomo originally
came to New York to take English classes and do research
for another screenplay, he departed from his original plan
after a few seminal New York experiences and decided to
make a film based upon his first summer in the city. Skyline
tells the story of a Spanish photographer, played beautifully
by Antonio Resines, who is looking for work in New York,
taking classes in English and seeking companionship. He
strikes out on all three and decides to return to Madrid,
leaving unanswered a phone call from Life magazine that holds
out the promise of a bright future for him in America.
Peter Besa called Skyline "a complete dud" as a comedy,
but another critic found it a "low-keyed comedy, very witty,"[4]
and enjoyable. Filmed on a shoestring budget, it represents
Colomo's return to the intimate filmmaking style of Paper
Tigers. [5]

With Skyline and I'm in a Crisis, Fernando Colomo
brings a new kind of energy to the Spanish cinema of the
1980s. His early films have served him well as an apprenticeship. With these two latest film works, Colomo has hit
his stride in comedy and one hopes he will continue in this
genre, looking for critical and commercial success here and
abroad.

Bibliography

Besa, Peter. "Review of La mano negra." Variety (Sept. 2,
    1980), 26.

Besa, Peter. "Review of Skyline." Variety (Oct. 12, 1983),
    18.

Besa, Peter. "Review of La línea del cielo (Skyline)."
    Variety (Oct. 12, 1983), 23.

Canby, Vincent. "Review of Skyline." New York Times
    (Apr. 3, 1984), C 15.

Marías, Miguel. "Review of Tigres de papel." Dirigido por No. 48, (Dec. 1977), 14-19.

Moskowitz. "Review of Estoy en crísis," Variety (Sept. 15, 1982), 16.

"Interview with Fernando Colomo." Dirigido por (Feb. 1978), 14-19.

"Se rueda Fernando Colomo." Casablanca (June 1982), 31-32.

Chapter 8

JAIME CHAVARRI (1943)

Filmography

Short Films: 1967--Run, Blancanieves, Run (8 mm.); 1969--Ginebra en los infiernos; 1971--Permanencia del arabesco, Estado de sitio, La Danza; 1973--Señales de la ventana; 1974--Rubens (TV), El mundo es como no es (TV); 1975--Vestida de tal (TV); 1976--El retablo de Dorian Gray (TV); 1978--Los episodios (TV); 1979--Pequeño planeta, La mujer sorda.

Feature Films: 1971--Pastel de sangre (as co-director); 1974--Los viajes escolares; 1976--El desencanto; 1977--A un Dios desconocido (To an Unknown God); 1980--Dedicatoria; 1983--Bearn (La sala de muñecas); 1984--Las bicicletas son para el verano.

     A contemporary of Fernando Colomo, Jaime Chavarrí was born in Madrid in 1943 and studied at the Colegio del Pilar. As a teenager, he became very interested in film and in those early years worked as an apprentice to many famous international film directors such as Carlos Saura and Victor Erice. He studied for a Law degree in Madrid and Zaragoza, and then, in 1968, entered the National Film School, leaving after two years before obtaining his degree.

     Chavarrí is a restless bachelor with much artistic talent. He worked for several years as Set Director on Victor Erice's film Los desafíos, on Peter Lillienthal's Jacob Von Gruten and Carlos Saura's Ana y los lobos, and with Erice again on El espíritu de la colmena before he directed his first feature film in 1974. Chavarrí also worked three years for Spanish television, where he raised enough money to film his own script of Los viajes escolares. Although he began his career making short films, which he considers all "likable failures,"[1] he prefers making feature films treating controversial themes. The story of Los viajes escolares (School Trips) centers around a very nervous and badly educated youngster who runs away from school to confront his eccentric, tyrannical family and discovers "death." Although Chavarrí's first film is fairly interesting, "the screenplay is marred by the director's inability to distinguish between farce and straight dramatic comedy."[2]

His next feature, El desencanto (Disenchantment) was lensed in the manner of a documentary. Essentially it is a family interview of the widow of Luis Panero, a famous Spanish Civil War poet, who talks about her husband's career. Her two sons also share with us some intimate details about what it is like to live with a renowned poet. The camera pans inside the rooms of the poet's home, then outside into the local bars. The widow is portrayed as a lovely, patient but long-suffering woman. Panero's sons are disturbingly different. The elder is eccentric--a pseudo-poet. The younger is committed only to himself. (He claims he never really knew his own father.) Like Jaime Camino's La vieja memoria, El desencanto is a long, long film based upon the testimony of family memories. La vieja memoria, though, is a thorough documentary revealing the historical perspectives of people whose life and death decisions affected the entire Spanish nation, while El desencanto is a film whose title is realized on a much smaller scale; it is an intimate testimony film, deftly and lovingly made with much care and feeling, but with few earth-shattering revelations.

Chavarrí's sensitivity to people and feelings is his most salient trait as a filmmaker. El desencanto conveys such astonishing impact because real people are talking about themselves in front of a camera and "convey with such lucidity and profundity an analysis of individual attitudes and class boundaries in Spain"[3] over the past thirty years. Up to this point, Chavarrí's films demonstrate his intention to find a personal esthetic through fictional feature films and pseudo-documentaries that are neither cinéma-verité nor candid camera. One critic called El desencanto "a moral striptease before Chavarrí's camera."[4]

It was in his third film that Chavarrí feels he did his best work although he felt that the "lack of clarity or ambiguousness was his own fault and not the Spanish censors."[5] When he decided to deal with the problem of homosexuality, formerly a taboo theme in Spanish cinema, he had no censorship restrictions from the government whatsoever. To an Unknown God is explicit about Federico García Lorca's sexual preferences. When the poet's sister, Isabel, saw the film at the Cannes Film Festival in 1977, she made no criticism of Chavarrí's handling of the homosexual theme. [6]

From Jaime Chavarrí's A un Dios desconocido (To an Unknown God, 1977), with Hector Alterio on the right.

To an Unknown God stars the popular Argentine actor Hector Alterio in the role of an actor-magician, an elegant homosexual who lives alone and has an occasional affair with a young politician who finds it more convenient in Madrid's high society to marry than assert his homosexuality. We follow José, the magician, through his daily experiences. He is a man romantically possessed and obsessed by his childhood in Granada during the outbreak of the Spanish Civil War. Now in his fifties, José returns to Granada and relives his childhood there (in flashback), a time when he fell in love with García Lorca and had a youthful affair with Lorca and/or one of Lorca's own lovers. Memories come flooding back to José, now in his fifties, of youthful conquests, of Lorca's murder at the hands of Franco's agents, and of his own early homosexual affairs. José's entire life is colored by his obsession with García Lorca, his "unknown God," to whom the film is dedicated.

During the course of the film, we travel twice to Granada with José: first, José revisits a woman who is also obsessed with García Lorca's memory, and steals a photograph of the boy with whom he had his first sexual encounter; later, José returns to Granada to a party in search of his youth and meets a pianist with whom he had sexual relations many years before but does not remember. When José returns to Madrid, he is a man tormented by his past, and in search of peace. Listening to a taped recording of García Lorca's famous Ode to Walt Whitman, he desires nothing more than to face the rest of his life in loneliness, although his recent lover, the politician, has returned to his bed and wants to continue their affair. José realizes that he is all alone in the world, alone with God.

Many European and Spanish critics were astonished by Chavarrí's frank, mature and unhysterical treatment of homosexuality. In fact the film is a totally mature exploration of an extremely controversial theme, never before dealt with by a Spanish director and aimed at a Spanish audience. There is not a single jarring note. "Chavarrí keeps the sex and poetry beautifully under control."[7] To an Unknown God "is lovely to look at, highly cultivated and poised."[8] This film is Chavarrí's best work to date. It is sensitive, allusive, graceful, intelligent, moving--in short, a masterpiece of Spanish cinema. It was the Grand Prize winner at the Chicago Film Fesitval of 1978 and was part of the American Film Institute series of Spanish films which traveled throughout North America in 1979-80. Hector Alterio also won the Best Actor award at the San Sebastián Film Festival in 1977 for his performance as José.

After To an Unknown God, Dedicatoria (1980) seems like a less ambitious film, on a much smaller scale. It was coolly received by Spanish film critics. Where Unknown God had controversial and symbolically international themes, Dedicatoria is so rooted to Iberia in its plot and acting that it will never cross the Spanish frontier.

It begins with a reporter seeking an interview with a

prisoner jailed somewhere outside of Madrid. He also interviews the prisoner's wife and daughter. The camera follows
his inquiry and his subsequent affairs, first with one woman
and then with the prisoner's daughter. In the film's final
scene, the daughter moves in to live with the reporter in his
Madrid apartment.

Chavarrí emphasizes the machismo of the Spanish
male, perhaps in deliberate contrast to the homosexual theme
of his earlier feature. However, Dedicatoria loses its focus:
is it a mystery about the prisoner he interviews or does it
deal with the sexual escapades of the reporter? Unlike other
Spanish films of the period, it shows women as aggressive
and independent. Upon the prisoner's death, the reporter
never uses his research for his "big" story. Despite exquisite exterior scenes shot in Segovia and lively urban
scenes in Madrid, Chavarrí's film is ambiguous. It never
clearly states the direction in which it is moving. We have
no conclusive ending. The actors are all very pleasing to
look at: José Luis Gómez plays the reporter, Amparo
Muñoz is the prisoner's daughter, and Luis Politti is suitably
taciturn and stolid as the prisoner who reveals little about
his life or the "mystery" within the film. One wonders if
the reporter's life was changed by his experiences on the
job and this may be the only realization that succeeds in this
strange but subtle film.

When not working on films, Chavarrí is assured of a
monthly salary check from Spanish television, where he films
shorts. 9 After Dedicatoria Chavarrí did some work in the
theatre and wrote a play which he considered a disaster, 10
but felt that his reputation as a filmmaker did not suffer as a
consequence. Chavarrí is an intellectual, always on the
move, seeking some new project. Still a bachelor, he is a
cosmopolite, has lived in Cambridge and speaks English
quite fluently. He enjoys the "new" freedom of the Spanish
cinema and believes To an Unknown God to be a significant
film that would never have been made if the Juan Carlos
government had not come to power. Formerly, the Spanish
public could not tolerate such an audacious film on a topic
such as homosexuality.

Chavarrí's most recent films, Bearn, subtitled La
sala de las muñecas (The Doll's Room, 1983) and Las
bicicletas son para el verano (Bicycles Are for the Summer,
1984) are as disparate thematically as their titles. Bearn
is a period costume drama set in Mallorca in 1865, starring

Fernando Rey, Angela Molina, Amparo Soler Leal and Imanol
Arias, and dealing with politics, family intrigues, incest and
clergy. Its tag line is: "Antes morir, que mezclar mi
sangre" (Before dying, let me mix my blood), which is as
ambiguous a line to advertise a film as has ever been written.
One hopes that the film will clarify this theme. Bicycles,
based upon a play which had a successful run in Madrid,
deals with the day-to-day experiences of a lower-middle-class
family during the Civil War. Even the excellent performances
of Fernando Fernán Gómez and Victoria Abril cannot save
this film from the banality of its themes. "One never feels
as close to the war as in Jaime Camino's The Long Vacations
of 36 or Mario Camus' The Beehive."[11] Perhaps Spanish
audiences are tiring of films about the Spanish Civil War.

One hopes that Chavarrí will continue to use his grace,
intelligence, depth of feeling, knowledge and sense of beauty
on more worthwhile projects.

Bibliography

Book: Semprún, Jorge. El desencanto (Madrid: Ed. Elías
Qurejeta, 1976) 144p. The entire screenplay.

Articles

Besa, Peter. "Review of El desencanto." Variety (Oct. 20,
1976), 39.

Besa, Peter. "Review of A un Dios desconocido." Variety
(Sept. 28, 1977), 24.

Besa, Peter. "Review of Dedicatoria." Variety (Mar. 28,
1980), 15.

Besa, Peter. "Review of Bearn." Variety (Apr. 27, 1983),
32.

Besa, Peter. "Review of Las bicicletas son para el verano."
Variety (Feb. 8, 1984), 20.

Canby, Vincent. "Homage to García Lorca." New York
Times (Apr. 7, 1978), 42.

Canby, Vincent. "Review of To an Unknown God." New York
Times (July 16, 1980), C 5. (Reprint of Apr. 7, 1978
review, NYT, C 7.)

"El cine desencantado de J. Chavarrí." Dirigido por No. 49 (1972), 44-56.

"Review of El desencanto." Cinema 2002 (Nov. 1976), 30-31; 44-45.

"Review of A un Dios desconocido." Cinema 2002 (Nov. 1977), 22-23.

"Una película exigente." Contracampo (Dec. 1980), 17-28.

Chapter 9

ANTONIO DROVE (1942)

Filmography

Short Features: 1966--¡Oh, sí, sí, tengo una mujer que está loca por mí!; La historia del suicida y la monjita; La primera comunión; 1967--La casa de brujas; 1969--Qué se puede hacer con una chica; 1973--Pura coincidencia (TV); 1974--Velásquez, la nobleza de la pintura (TV); La gran

Antonio Drove (center) directing Charles Denner (l.) and José Luis López Vásquez on the set of La verdad Sobre el caso Savolta (1978).

batalla de Andalucía (TV); 1975--Aquí durmió Carlos III (TV); El destino de Antonio Navajo.

Feature Films: 1974--Tocata y fuga de Lolita; Mi mujer es muy decente dentro de lo que cabe; 1976--Nosotros que fuimos tan felices; 1978-79--La verdad sobre el caso Savolta (The Truth About the Savolta Affair).

Antonio Drove is a former engineering student and like so many other young film directors of his generation, he became disenchanted with his chosen profession and chose filmmaking instead. Drove was born in Madrid on November 1, 1942. Married to a Catalonian woman and with two small children, he is of Scotch-English-Spanish descent although the considers himself a true madrileño. He joined the National Film School in 1966 and graduated two years later. Drove began his film career with a great number of short subjects and continues to work in Spanish television as a director of short subjects and a script writer. He is very well acquainted with international cinema and feels that D.W. Griffith, Fritz Lang and Jean Renoir have been the most formidable influences upon his own career. Drove considers himself one of the most "political" filmmakers in Spain today and alluded to a four-day strike in the television industry, the first ever in Spain, which he initiated.[1] Drove considers himself a man of strong convictions and prefers to work in "revisionist" cinema, political films that change one's thinking.

Of all his short features and films he says he enjoyed doing only two: La caza de brujas (Witch Hunt) and his most widely known feature, La verdad sobre el caso Savolta (The Truth About the Savolta Affair.) Drove considers Savolta an "epic" film, though not in the same way one considers David O. Selznick's Gone With the Wind an epic. Savolta is a political statement against tyranny, not just an entertainment.[2]

While Drove emphasized his serious side, his comic nature is also evident in all pre-Savolta films. Drove admits his eclecticism, and his debt especially to Ernst Lubitsch, Howard Hawks and Billy Wilder. He tried, with partial success, to imitate the latter's rapid-fire dialogue and unlikely comical situations in some of his early films, although Drove admits he has difficulties directing some of his actors. Having seen several of Drove's comedies, I much prefer to discuss his serious films, especially La verdad sobre el caso Savolta.

Scenes from <u>La verdad sobre el caso Savolta</u> (1978). At top, Stefania Sandrelli and Ovidi Montllor. Below, the takeover of the munitions factory.

In further scenes from <u>La verdad sobre el caso Savolta</u>, a young factory worker (above) and the cowardly accountant (below).

Because many of Drove's films deal with political themes, he sometimes finds himself in conflict with the government. Under the Franco regime, he was arrested several times--once in Oviedo for showing The Tale of the Suicide & the Nun (1966) and when The Witch Hunt (1967) was shown publicly, the National Film School banned it, called it "one of the grimmest documentaries on moral repression ever filmed in Spain."[3] These early short films emphasize Drove's continual political entanglements with the Franco regime. Amparo Muñoz in Tocata y fuga de Lolita was the first actress to remove her brassiere in a Spanish film, to the chagrin of the Franco regime, ensuring the film's commercial success. Because of his revisionist ideas in a TV film entitled La gran batalla de Andalucia, which proselytized for collective action against tyranny, his next TV film, El destino de Antonio Navajo, was released with a mutilated soundtrack, forcing Drove to withdraw his name from the credits. Savolta, a French-Italian-Spanish co-production, is Drove's first film which has gone uncensored in Spain and for which he feels totally responsible. He still had to face some adversities while filming it--a four-month strike of technicians when the producers tried to remove Drove as director for "unknown" reasons. Drove has suffered a series of harassments in his professional life because he is essentially honest and wanted to preserve his ideal of telling a truthful story on the screen. Savolta is the result of his uncompromising attitude and artistic courage.

La verdad sobre el caso Savolta, shot in color and Cinemascope, is based upon real events. Although it is freely based upon a novel by Eduardo Mendoza, Drove and Antonio Larreta wrote the script, emphasizing the true historical events which took place in Barcelona between 1917 and 1923. Savolta is a Catalan munitions manufacturer who is trying to obtain war contracts with both French and German governments before World War I. The factory workers are treated badly by the Savolta family and labor strikes ensue. The labor unions urge reforms but have no leverage in obtaining them until a journalist named Pajarito (remarkably well-played by José Luis López Vásquez) obtains secret information from Savolta's accountant that a French representative of the firm, Leprince, played calculatingly by French star Charles Denner, has been selling arms secretly to the Germans as well as smuggling war materials and falsifying bills. Leprince is the real Machiavelli of the plot since it is he who orders the deaths of the strike leaders and later kills Savolta himself, realizing the strikers will be blamed for the murders. Leprince extracts all the pertinent information from the journalist about

Concha Velasco in Antonio Drove's Mi mujer es muy decente... (1974)

incriminating documents, proving that Savolta had sold arms
to the Germans. When the journalist's wife discovers that
her husband is blamed and called a traitor, she commits
suicide and her lover, played unctuously by Ovidi Montllor,
becomes Leprince's ambitious number one henchman. Savolta
himself loses control because of the demands of the anarchist
unions, although it is actually due to Leprince's plotting to
wrest total control of the company.

The film concludes with a bloodbath caused by the
murder of union leaders by paid thugs, sometime between
the end of World War I and the imminent dictatorship of
Primo de Rivera in Spain, 1931. Leprince and his henchman,
Miranda, remain on the periphery of the action, although they
are directly responsible for the murders of union leaders.
In one wonderful scene, Miranda wants to kill Leprince for
the havoc he has wreaked in his own personal life while both
are touring the Savolta munitions factory, but Leprince talks
Miranda out of shooting him--to their mutual advantage.
Another marvelous scene takes place during a masked ball
at Savolta's home. (Savolta is beautifully played by the
Italian actor Omero Antonutti.) Leprince is dressed as
Pierrot and is engaged to Savolta's daughter. Savolta is
dressed as Julius Caesar, suitably robed for his demise,
and Miranda wears the appropriate costume of a fifteenth-
century inquisitioner under Torquemada's aegis.

The Truth of the Savolta Affair is a wonderful political
thriller, rich in color, action, character development and
period detail, conceived much in the manner of Costa-Gavras'
films Z or State of Siege or Missing. Drove insists he stayed
as close to the historical events as possible and did not kill
off the villains because, "historically, things were not really
like that. Secondly, I did not want an individual solution
and thirdly, it would have left everyone free of worry."[4]
Drove's intent was to depict in Savolta the dangerous disguise
of fascism--to show that fascists are human beings who can
also be villains, not necessarily big political criminals but
perhaps the perpetrators of big political crimes. Drove's
aim is to have audiences recognize fascism and its instiga-
tors, and to persuade the public to guard against fascism in
the future. Unlike the film noir, where crime is considered
big business, Drove believes Savolta shows how big business
can become a crime. His film ends with the defeat of the
Worker's Movement and the rise of fascism. The film
corroborates his historical conclusion but it opposes the very
ideology it upholds. The film ends with a quotation from

The new sexual freedom: Amparo Muñoz and Arturo Fernandez in Drove's Tocata y fuga de Lolita (1974).

Bertold Brecht: "Only violence can help where violence is the rule." One must fight fire with fire. Drove reminds Spaniards and his viewers that they must never be suborned by fascism. The Spaniards had been living under a Fascistic government from 1931 to 1975. Drove's disputes with his producers over the film's ideological center almost caused him to be fired. In fact, Argentine director Diego Santillán also worked on several scenes while Drove argued to retain his political viewpoint. The result is an intelligent and effective film which advances Drove's anti-fascist views and keeps his integrity intact, testifying to his talent as one of Spain's leading, most serious, politically-engagé directors.

Bibliography

Besa, Peter. "Review of La verdad sobre el caso Savolta." Variety (May 28, 1980), 14.

Llinas, Francesc. "Nunca estuvimos en el rio Misisipí: Entrevista con Drove." Contracampo (May, 1980), 17-33.

Marias, Miguel. "Entrevista con A. Drove." Dirigido por (Feb. 1975), 22-27.

Santos-Zunzunegui, L. "La reforma, el fascismo y las causas evitables." Contracampo (May 1980), 13-16.

"Drove: Hacer cine para aprende a vivir." Cinema 2002 (Apr. 1980), 60-64.

Chapter 10

VICTOR ERICE (1940)

Filmography

Short Films: 1961--En la terraza; 1962--Entrevías, Páginas de un diario perdido; 1963--Los días perdidos; 1968--Al final de la tarde.

Feature films: 1968--Los desafíos (co-directed by Claudio Guerin Hill & José Luis Egea); 1973--El espíritu de la colmena (The Spirit of the Beehive); 1983--El sur (The South).

He was born in the Basque provinces in the small town of Carranza in 1940, but very little else is known about Victor Erice's childhood or teenage years. In 1960, he came to Madrid and entered the National Film School, where he completed several short films (listed above). Besides studying Political Science, he occasionally wrote film criticism for two leading Spanish magazines, Nuestro cine and Cuadernos de arte y pensamiento. He finally graduated from film school in 1968. The last short he made there was entitled Al final de la tarde.

Erice is a prolific script writer, and has collaborated with Antonio Eceiza on El próximo otoño and with Miguel Picazo on Oscuros sueños de agosto. Between feature films, Erice works for Spanish television, occasionally turning out a feature program, but is currently directing commercials, which guarantee him a regular monthly salary.

When his first feature film was released in 1973, The Spirit of the Beehive created a sensation among Spanish audiences and intellectuals. Erice was highly touted as a leader among Spain's newer young, intellectual filmmakers, including Alvaro del Amo and Jaime Chavarrí. "The film

Victor Erice (photo courtesy Filmoteca Nacional, Madrid).

followed Erice's promising but rather incoherent sketch in
Los desafíos, and its maturity and narrative control came
as a surprise."[1]

Among other Spanish filmmakers, Erice has the reputation of a loner. He is the most secretive of film directors.
He may work in publicity and TV commercials, but demands
absolute privacy concerning his personal and professional life.
I was fortunate to interview him when he promised to send
me the published screenplay of Beehive, which also contains
one of the two published interviews he has granted any reporter or film scholar in Spain.[2]

The Spirit of the Beehive most deservedly won First
Prize at the San Sebastián Film Festival in 1973. At the
Ninth Chicago Film Festival, it was awarded the Silver Hugo

Ana Torrent (r.) and Isabel Telleria in Victor Erice's The Spirit of the Beehive (1973).

for "its vivid unsentimental evocation of the world of child-hood and its masterly direction of child performers."[3]

It is not easy to summarize the complex plot of Beehive, since the film may be read on several levels. The action is set in a remote Castilian village in 1940, shortly after the Spanish Civil War. Reminders of the war are seen everywhere, although the village itself was left unscathed. Every Sunday, a traveling movie exhibitor arrives with a new Hollywood film; this week it is James Whale's Frankenstein, the 1932 black-and-white Universal production starring Boris Karloff. When the film is shown at a local meeting hall on a small screen, the entire town attends; the streets are entirely deserted. The audience consists mostly of old women and children. Among them is Isabel, age ten, and her sister, Ana, age seven. During the film Ana asks Isabel why the monster kills the little girl and why he dies at the end. Isabel answers, somewhat elaborately, that the monster is a spirit which she can

summon anytime just by saying the right words. What begins as a figment of Isabel's imagination becomes a reality
for Ana. Isabel had made up the convoluted story for Ana
out of boredom more than maliciousness and boredom with
provincial life is one of the film's essential themes. We become acquainted with Isabel and Ana's parents very quickly.
They are an upper-middle class family who fled from a
larger estate (never identified) and brought a few treasured
possessions with them, especially a charming timepiece
which the father, Fernando, fondles throughout the film
until it disappears. The mother, Teresa, spends her days
writing long letters to her young lover, now in the army,
but who is probably dead. Fernando's only occupation of
sorts is tending his bees and keeping a journal in which he
tries to sort out the "unsortable" facts of man's existence.
"He keeps away from actually participating in life by dealing
in metaphors, pondering at length a quotation from Maeter-
linck's Life of the Bee. "[4]

Clearly, Fernando and Teresa are clandestine hermits,
living in a beautiful, austere farmhouse that once was a place
they may have come to for vacations with their two young
daughters. Their sense of isolation from their own daughters
and from each other is heart-rending. Along with the geographical devastation of war all around them, there is the
physical shabbiness and scarcity of post-Civil War Spain,
a country of widows and burnt-out survivors. Ana and Isabel
are growing up in this milieu and live among these shadows
and dreams.

The rest of the film deals with Ana's search for her
own imagination, her own mystery, her own spirit. Initially
looking for the Frankenstein monster, she discovers at one
point an army deserter in an abandoned house way out in the
country. She brings him food, bandages and her father's
coat for warmth, with the latter's favorite chiming pocket
watch still in the coat. When the deserter is shot and the
father is called by the local Civil Guard to reclaim his
possessions, he interrogates his daughters. Ana cannot
bring herself to tell the truth, decides to run away, and many
hours later, after an all-night search by the townspeople,
she is found sleeping, silent and withdrawn. According to
the town's local doctor, Ana had experienced some sort of
nervous breakdown, but with rest, love and medication, she
will soon be in good health once again. Her sister Isabel
feels guilty for scaring Ana with malicious tales about the
Frankenstein monster. However, as Ana seems to recuperate,

she realizes that she can summon the monster as she did
once before, the night of her fateful breakdown. "In the
film's closing scene, Ana exorcises her sadness, advances
to the window, looks up at the baleful moon and remembers
she has the power to call Frankenstein back."[5]

Ana Torrent as Ana gives probably the most extraordinary performance by a child actress ever seen in international cinema. "With her woebegone drawn face and
rather petulant air, she completely carries such difficult
moments as her meeting with the benevolent monster at
night."[6] "Ana responds to the demands of Erice's direction
with remarkable feeling."[7]

The Spirit of the Beehive is a lyrical film whose style
may be characterized as ambiguous and elliptical. Using
the camera and color with a painter's eye, Erice combines
a marvelous vision of childhood with a gently poetic visual-
ization of a dream world. The film's comparison with René
Clement's Jeux interdits (Forbidden Games) is entirely
natural. But unlike Clement's film, Spirit's atmospheric
quality and blending of the macabre with the gentle, its un-
forgettable images, as beautiful and dark as a Goya painting,
transform this film into a work of art that could come only
from Spain. The genius displayed in the photography by the
late Luis Cuadrado, the carefully underlit scenes that give
even sunny days a darkening quality, are touches of genius
attributable to both Cuadrado and Erice. Erice suggests
more than he ever tells us about his own past and his post-
Civil War childhood experiences in the Basque country. On
occasion the film's symbolism may be confusing but Spirit
is a complex film and possesses its viewers completely.
Erice's first film demonstrates great directorial control,
like the early work of Josef Von Sternberg, for which he
shows much admiration and passion.[8] Like Von Sternberg,
Erice has reconstructed a magical world of childhood, of
murmured words and whispers, of beautiful imagery, stark
emotions, haunting dreams, of isolation and loneliness,
dramatic intensity and spiritual emptiness and decay that
may be the pervasive symbol of the entire Spanish nation
for 1973.

"The Spirit of the Beehive was the first film in more
than thirty years to offer a truthful view of the oppressive
atmosphere of post-war Spain as seen from the loser's
point of view."[9] Erice himself has said of the film: "It is
not a narrative film, but rather a work which has a

fundamentally lyrical, musical structure and whose images lie deep in the very heart of mythical experience. "[10]

Interpreting the film on a different level, Michel Pérez of Le Quotidien de Paris offered the following comments: "The two little girls naturally live around monsters. Their innocence is their shield against fear, in an existence where death is as pervasive as life. . . . Erice shows us the real monsters. Ignome is the most hideous one; resignation and humility are very close behind. "[11] One must remember that Erice had to contend with censorship problems while Spirit was being filmed. Despite Michel Pérez's ideological interpretation of this film, Spirit indeed profits from the ambiguity within its scenario, the elliptical nature of its style and the obliqueness of its commentaries. Erice is a man of great sensitivity and it would have seemed rude for him to spell out literally his "political" intentions. Spirit of the Beehive succeeds as a work of art, working within the constraints of Spanish censorship, but transcending both geographical and intellectual boundaries.

Erice's second feature film, El sur (The South, 1983) opened to successful reviews in Madrid and New York ten years later at the 1983 Festival of Spanish Films on November 3 at the Guild Theatre. Starring Omero Antonutti, Lola Cardona and Rafaela Aparicio, it deals once again in Erice's elliptical style with the pains of childhood, memory and the Spanish Civil War. It is a masterful drama and confirms Erice as a major talent in Spanish cinema. As a result of some cuts made by the producer, Elías Querejeta, Erice supposedly never finished the film, but Querejeta edited the footage and released it under the director's name. [12]

El sur is a richly textured film about a girl's relationship with her father from pre-adolesence to her teenage years. We discover that her father left the south because of ideological differences over the Civil War. The film concentrates on developing the relationship between father and daughter, revealing the father's past love affair with an actress, his disillusion living in the north, his suicide. Left with her mother, Estrella, the daughter decides to go south, to visit her grandparents and aunts and perhaps to penetrate the mysteries behind her father's strange behavior. El sur extends the lyricism of Spirit of the Beehive into the 1980s and confirms Victor Erice as a rare directorial talent of contemporary Spanish cinema.

Iciar Bollain in a scene from Erice's El Sur (The South, 1983).

Bibliography

Besa, Peter. "San Sebastian Films Reviewed." Variety (Oct. 3, 1973), 18.

Besa, Peter. "Review of Spirit of the Beehive." Variety (Sept. 22, 1976), 14.

Besa, Peter. "Review of El sur." Variety (June 1, 1983), 18.

Bodeen, Dwight. "Review of El espíritu de la colmena." Films in Review (November 1976), 569.

Canby, Vincent. "A Perilous Country." New York Times (Sept. 24, 1976), C 8.

Genover, Jaume. "Review of El espíritu de la colmena." Dirigido por (Jan. 1974), 25.

McGuiness, Richard. "Review of The Spirit of the Beehive."
Thousand Eyes (Oct. 1976), 8.

Molina-Foix, Vicente. "Entretien avec Victor Erice."
Positif (Feb. 1984), 47-51.

Montero, Rosa. "Interview with Victor Erice." Jano (Nov.
16, 1973), 101-102, 105.

Paranagua, Paulo Antonio. "La solitude de Victor Erice."
Positif (Feb. 1984), 46.

Winsten, Archer. "Beautifully Constructed Beehive." New
York Post (Sept. 24, 1976), 46.

"Review of Los días perdidos." Film Ideal (Oct. 1963), 67.

"Review of The Spirit of the Beehive." Sight & Sound (Winter
1973-74), 37.

"A Great Film We May Never See." New York Times (Sept.
12, 1976), 18.

Screenplay

Fernández Santos, Angel & Erice, Victor. El espíritu de la
colmena. (Madrid: Ed. Elías Querejeta, 1976) 165 pages.

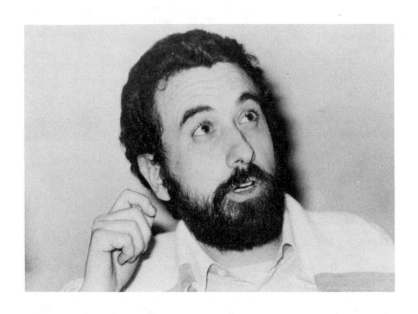

Chapter 11

JOSE LUIS GARCI (1944)

Filmography

Short Films; 1974--Al fútbol; 1975--Mi Marilyn; 1976--
Tiempo de gente a cobardada; 1980--Alfonso Sánchez.

Feature Films: 1976--Asignatura pendiente; 1977--Sólos en
la madrugada; 1979--Las verdes praderas; 1981--El Crack
(The Crack); 1982--Volver a empezar (To Begin Again or
Begin the Beguine); 1983--El Crack Dos; 1984--Sesión continua
(Double Feature).

Born in Madrid in 1944, the multi-talented José Luis
Garcí began his career first as a film critic, then turned to
scriptwriting and finally became a director of short films
and, later, feature films. Self-taught, he never attended
any film school and is probably one of the youngest, most
prolific, widely commercial and successful young Spanish

Above, José Luis Garcí (photo courtesy of the director).

film directors known in Europe and abroad. In fact, his
recent feature, Volver a empezar (1982), won the Academy
Award for Best Foreign Film in 1983, according him
international accolades. When Garcí went up to the podium
to collect his "Oscar," he proclaimed that "Oscar" was a
long time in coming. Garcí is a major commercial talent
on the way up to future success. He has always felt he
prefers to make "movies, not films."[1] Adhering to Pauline
Kael's definitions of movies vs. cinema, Garcí is interested
in making movies for the masses, not the cinemaphiles or
intellectuals, and prefers commercial success to artistic
failure.[2] He always tries to reach the mass audience. His
last three films are all crowd pleasers. El Crack (Parts I
and II) are send-ups of the old popular film noir detective
mysteries, and To Begin Again is a sentimental, nostalgic
love story for adults which is reminiscent of the best Hollywood romantic dramas of the 1930s and 1940s. Garcí himself is a movie buff who knows American films well; at the
same time, he is a very clever technician and businessman
who knows how to market successfully a totally commercial
product based upon tried and tested cinematic formulas.

Married and the father of two daughters, Garcí complains he has not enough time for his family because of the
extremely busy schedule he sets for himself.[3] He usually
prepares a film in about one year, although the actual shooting of scenes may take between four and six weeks. (It takes
him at least six months to prepare the script.) He believes
in rehearsing his actors and never has had problems directing. Garcí prefers to remake the classical films of yesteryear and admits that El Crack was his own homage to the
film noir of the 1940s; he dedicated it to Dashiell Hammett.

Garcí is a cosmopolitan director who usually prefers
to shoot his films abroad. Besides filming in Madrid, he has
also used New York and San Francisco for locales. Garcí
adores Hollywood and the United States and would prefer to
live in New York. "Movies are like an emotion for me, a
world of images where mythologies are mixed surprisingly
with new realities."[4] Garcí's favorite directors are John
Ford, Alfred Hitchcock, Howard Hawks, Ernst Lubitsch,
Billy Wilder, Jean Renoir, Carl Dreyer, Luis Berlanga, and
among his favorite films are Casablanca, Notorious, The Man
Who Shot Liberty Valance and Sunset Boulevard. Garcí would
like to see other Spanish directors try to revive the old
successful Hollywood themes, not just as a tribute to the
directors of yesteryear but so that Spaniards themselves

might discover through eclecticism their own talent and direction in their own unique national cinema.

A review of Garcí's early days as a film critic and prize-winning short story writer demonstrates their impact on his career. Having worked as an editor for Signo and Cine estudio magazines, as well as Aún, SP and Reseña, Garcí became well known in the Spanish film industry as a specialist in, and a fervent admirer of, Hollywood "movies." In fact, in 1969, he was awarded a prize by the Círculo de escritores cinematográficos for his articles on film and film criticism.

Among Garcí's circle of interests is his propensity for science fiction. In 1970, he published his first book of short stories entitled Bibidibabidibí, and in 1971, a critical book entitled Ray Bradbury, humanista del futuro. Another short story, "Adam Blake," appeared in 1972 and a critical film work, Cine de ciencia ficción, in 1973. While writing screenplays, Garcí also pursues his other creative and critical talents, publishing, for example, La Gioconda está triste y otras extrañas historias, a fictional work. In June 1981, he won a $7500 prize (The Golden Gate Award) for a six-page short story entitled "Los mejores años de nuestra vida," competing with more than four thousand writers.

No stranger to awards, he won an American television Emmy in 1973 for his TV script entitled La cabina. All his previous television scripts were well received and were a prelude to the scriptwriting he did during the mid-1970s and early 1980s. Of the three short films he made, Mi Marilyn is Garcí's biggest commercial success and his own personal favorite. A film biography of the late Marilyn Monroe, it is the most widely exhibited short film in the history of Spanish cinema; it won Garcí ten international film prizes.

Garcí's first feature film, Asignatura pendiente, became a sociological phenomenon in Spain. It broke all box-office records there as well as in Mexico and Argentina, and was described as the most "sincere" movie ever made in Spain. The plot of Garcí's auspicious debut film is deceptively simple. Two old school friends meet. José Sacristán plays a pushy lawyer, married, with one son, and bored with his wife. Fiorella Faltoyana plays the role of a true ama de casa (housewife) who is also bored with her own husband and two daughters. They manage to meet clandestinely for two days, rent an apartment and tell each other

Two scenes from Garcí's <u>Asignatura pendiente</u> (<u>Exam Pending</u>, 1976). Below, Fiorella Faltoyano and José Sacristán.

their problems and their dreams while they make love against the background of an endless supply of their favorite records.

Asignatura pendiente may have been an important film in its time because of the apertura, or new freedoms, opened up by Spanish politics after Franco's death. Nostalgia, however, is not enough to save the friendship or the respective marriages of Sacristán and Faltoyana. Divorce laws were non-existent in Spain at this time and therefore, couples either separated or maintained the status quo. The film seemed too long, too trite, and was filled with too much dialogue. However, it was a decided force which opened the way for a more authentic cinema, a more spontaneous, direct approach to filming contemporary problems. In my view, though, it still cannot be considered in any way a classic of modern Spanish cinema despite its commercial success.

Sólos a la madrugada (Alone at Dawn, 1978) uses the same actor, José Sacristán, and continues the theme of the apertura--the story of the transition in Spain from Francoist government to democracy. It was banned in Spain because of its pernicious nihilism and I was unable to see it or its successor, Las verdes praderas (The Green Meadows, 1979). Garcí called these films his "cinema of emotions with political backgrounds. "[5]

My own association with Garcí and his career began in 1981 when El Crack was running on Madrid's Gran Vía. Having been brought up in America and the tradition of the film noir of the 1940s and 1950s, it was exciting for me to see his first Spanish crime thriller in Madrid. El Crack is Garcí's most imitative, eclectic American film, and his most commercial. A private detective, Alfredo Landa, is initially hired to find the daughter of a dying man. She turns out to be a prostitute working in a local massage parlor. The story becomes convoluted as the detective's personal affairs (he is dating a psychological therapist played by Maria Casanova while playing father to her seven-year-old daughter) become confused with the prostitute's problems. The prostitute apparently doubles as a messenger used by a high-level crime organization whose headquarters are in New York. When the therapist's daughter is killed by a bomb planted in the detective's car (compare Jocelyn Brando's demise in Fritz Lang's The Big Heat), Landa leaves for New York to take revenge. He murders the head of the Syndicate at an Italian restaurant on Manhattan's East side and tells the

Spanish gunsel who planted the bomb that he has tied three
pieces of ham, not explosives, to his chest, to keep the
gunman out of harm's way. As the gunsel undoes the bandages, an explosion is heard in the motel room at Kennedy
Airport as Landa boards a flight for his return to Madrid.
At home for Christmas, the detective renews his affair with
the therapist, who no longer blames him for her daughter's
death.

Alfredo Landa is excellent in his macho "little-guy"
role as the detective. His penetrating stare truly mesmer-
izes his victims. "The picture comes across as a charming
homage to American filmmakers of the 1940s."[6] Garcí succeeds in capturing the charm of downtown Madrid at night.
His panoramas, pans, and fadeouts are all reminiscent of
the great American cameramen of 1940s crime films, and a
nostalgic musical theme highlighting the thrill of New York
and Madrid city skylines revives the romanticism of a lonely
detective's life in the jungle of urban life. The film is
perfectly orchestrated, contains well-defined characters and
is deftly played by its performers.

Although El Crack and its sequel have not yet been
shown in the United States, Garcí's 1982 production, for
which he won the Academy Award, has made him one of the
most widely known and sought-after Spanish filmmakers.
Volver a empezar (To Begin Again) "is a top-notch film, one
of the best made in Spain recently, and a natural for the
international festival circuit."[7] Titled Begin the Beguine
in Spain, it was an international success, not totally to my
liking, but another commercial crowd pleaser. It is an
extremely sentimental film about the Spanish youth of the
1930s who never got the chance to fulfill their romantic
dreams because of the Civil War. Dedicating the film to
this group of Spaniards and to lovers everywhere, Garcí tells
the story of a Spanish professor (capably played by Antonio
Ferrandis) who returns to Gijón in Northern Spain to visit an
old friend, a doctor named Roxú, and his first love, Elena
(brilliantly played by Encarna Paso), with whom he danced
to Cole Porter's famous song "Begin the Beguine" in 1936.
She was his "Ginger" (Rogers) and he was her "Fred"
(Astaire). During the war, Antonio left for America and
vowed never to return until Franco left the seat of the Spanish government. When Antonio returns to Gijón, the new
King, Juan Carlos, telephones him at the small hotel in
which he is staying, creating quite a stir. He meets Elena,
his former teenage sweetheart, at the Art Gallery she runs

José Luis Garcí (above and opposite) directing four scenes from <u>El Crack</u> (1981).

Antonio Ferrandis and Encarna Paso in scene from Garcí's
Volver a empezar (1982).

and they spend many, many romantic moments together.
Antonio is divorced and has two grown-up sons living in
America. Elena admits that she married a man she did not
love and was in love with another man who could not leave
his wife.

Throughout the film, the college professor is taking
some mysterious medication, probably pain killers. In one
amusing exchange with Elena, he makes fun of Americans,
saying, "Everyone there is on some kind of pill." He con-
fides his illness to his boyhood doctor-friend Roxú, and the
latter realizes that Antonio has terminal cancer and about
six months left to live. This is why Antonio wanted to return to his roots. He dances with Elena to the Cole Porter
theme that haunts every frame of this film, although there
are some other musical references to Pachabel as well as
to other sentimental melodies. Having spent the night with
Elena, he returns to Berkeley, awaiting the inevitable. Before he leaves, Elena gives him a package to open when he
arrives at his apartment in San Francisco over-looking the
Golden Gate Bridge. The package contains some nostalgic
photos of Elena and Antonio circa 1936 and the 78 rpm record
of Artie Shaw's version of "Begin the Beguine."

Despite its predictable conclusion, Volver a empezar
is a lovely film, astonishingly sentimental and dedicated to

love and lovers over thirty. The film has some outstanding performances, a sensitive script and flawless direction, cinematography and editing. These virtues won it the Academy Award for Best Foreign Film of 1983. However, the story is maudlin, and Garcí's handling of the script teeters on the edge of the lachrymose. Nevertheless, it was a big commercial success in the United States and has enjoyed a first-run engagement in Madrid for nearly two years.

Garcí's next project was tentatively entitled Areta investigación and he would tell me no more about it other than the title.[8] Apparently he decided to resurrect his famous detective from El Crack and make a sequel, El Crack Dos, in the manner of the successive Rocky films. Although El Crack Dos opened to less than rave reviews in Madrid in August of 1983, Areta (Alberto Landa) still has a huge following in Madrid. Unlike its predecessor, "Garcí indulges himself in magnificent but pointless mood shots of Madrid's skyline."[9] Landa repeats his role, the detective Garcí shaped from the Hammett mold. Garcí adds a homosexual ambience to a story that has little irony or humor and that probably will not be as successful as El Crack Uno.

Judging from his latest commercial successes, Garcí will probably continue making "movies," not "films." He is mass-oriented, a director of undeniable youth, energy and talent. His entire career is yet to be fully evaluated.

Bibliography

Besa, Peter. "Review of Asignatura pendiente." Variety (Aug. 17, 1977), 20.

Besa, Peter. "Review of Sólos en la madrugada." Variety (Apr. 26, 1978), 19.

Besa, Peter. "Review of El Crack." Variety (Apr. 22, 1981), 26.

Besa, Peter. "Review of Volver a empezar." Variety (Apr. 14, 1982), 18.

Besa, Peter. "Review of El Crack Dos." Variety (Aug. 31, 1983), 18.

Besa, Peter. "Review of Sesión Contínua." Variety (Aug. 8, 1984), 14.

Hidalgo, Miguel. "Entrevista con J. L. Garcí." Cinema 2002 (Mar. 1979), 46-51.

Rentero, J.C. "Entrevista con J. L. Garcí." Dirigido por No. 55, 48-56.

"En la cuesta de la ola: J. L. Garcí." Diario (Dec. 25, 1981), 38-39.

Chapter 12

ANTONIO GIMENEZ-RICO (1938)

Filmography

1966--Mañana de domingo; 1968--El hueso; 1969--El cronicón;
1972--¿Es Vd. mi padre?; 1976--Retrato de familia (Family
Portrait); 1977--Al fin, solos, pero...; 1978--Del amor y la
muerte; 1983--Vestida de azul (Dressed in Blue).

Antonio Giménez-Rico was born in Burgos on October
20, 1938 and holds a Law degree from the University of Val-
ladolid, where he also majored in Journalism. He first became interested in film at the university, where he was director of the film club. He also worked at the university
theatre, became a founder of the Radio Popular program and
began writing film criticism for the magazine Cine estudio.
Criticism led to writing screenplays which in turn gave him
the opportunity to direct his first short subject, Crónica, in
1965 after he had made some commercial and industrial films.

Since 1970, Giménez-Rico has worked diligently for
Spanish television, directing over forty shows in the series
Crónica de un pueblo, among others. Married and with one
child, Giménez-Rico prefers to write the screenplays for his
own films; the movie industry is suffering from a lack of
writing talent and a lack of producers who know how to market
their product.[1] Although he prefers to direct feature films,
Giménez-Rico must work in television in order to earn a
regular living.

His first film, Mañana de domingo, was made in 1966,
"an amateur effort."[2] His favorite film from his early years
is Huesos (1968), in which he demonstrated that he could develop comical themes with a certain cold technical skill. El
cronicón (1969) is a corrosive film utilizing the Catholic rulers
Ferdinand and Isabella as a motif to criticize modern Spanish
society. The Spanish censors mutilated the film in such a way

Two scenes from Giménez-Rico's Retrato de familia (Family Portrait, 1976). Above, Monica Randall with Antonio Ferrandis. Below, Randall embraces Miguel Bose.

that Giménez-Rico's critical points were lost to the public. ¿Es Vd. mi padre?, according to the director, was a "total disaster. "[3] Regarding his film work up to 1976, Giménez-Rico feels his motion pictures revolve around two polarities --humor and melodrama.

Retrato de familia (Family Portrait) was made in 1976 and Giménez-Rico considers it his best-known film, in and outside of Spain. It usually takes five to six weeks to shoot any of his films. Regarding style, Rico considers himself a realist and a practitioner of realist cinema, calling himself "the Dickens of Spain."[4] Retrato is based upon the celebrated novel by Miguel Delibes, Mi hijo idolatrado, Sisí (My Adored Son, Sisí). It is Giménez-Rico's major critical and commercial success to date. Filmed in the director's home city of Burgos, it is the story of the Rubes, a family which is enduring the rigors of Civil War in a village of Castilla la Vieja, Caceres, in 1936. The father, Cecilio (played by Antonio Ferrandis), is a roué in love with another woman, Paulina (played by Monica Randall), although he lives with his wife (played by Amaparo Soler Leal) and his teenage son (Miguel Bose in his acting debut). His wife hates the thought of sexuality in their marriage. Their son notes his parents' sexual frustrations but must experience his own initiation into the mysteries of love and sex. We watch him grow, mature, compete with his father for the attentions and sexual favors of the local actresses in Burgos.

One day, quite by chance, Sisí meets Paulina, his father's more or less discarded lover, and they begin a tumultuous affair. Sisí is then inducted into the army and goes off to war. News of his death arrives quickly. Apparently Sisí was killed by a land mine while driving an army truck. His father wants his wife to bear him another son, but she refuses. The old man, broken-hearted by Sisí's death, returns to his mistress, Paulina, who tells him she is pregnant by his son. With no legal heir, the elder Cecilio Rubes, desperate, jumps off his mistress's balcony and commits suicide. Paulina had always wanted the elder Rubes' child but is now content with having one sired by his son.

Rich in historical detail, settings and costumes, Family Portrait is a marvelous film, capturing the spirit of Castille's provincial life during the 1930s. Miguel Bose, son of actress Lucia Bose and bullfighter Luís Dominguín, is superb as Sisí, the spoiled and handsome señorito who literally seduces every woman he meets. We watch him as a child go out on his first date. At the death of his grandmother, he

arrives late to the funeral and is summarily slapped by his
father for lack of respect. Sisí slaps his father in return,
demonstrating his egocentric character and a total lack of
respect for family and authority, symbolic of the lack of
authority during this period of Civil War.

Giménez-Rico is adept at developing the entire group
of characters who live in the apartment house, especially
Sisí's next-door neighbors. Sisí is infatuated with the "piano-
playing" daughter whom he genuinely respects and loves.
When he is killed, she accepts his death as part of a "Great
Cause," elevating his demise politically. Sisí's father cannot accept this explanation and rails against the Nationalist
armies under Franco. Family Portrait is one of the first
films to show resentment against the winning side. Also,
there are several sensual sexual scenes and scenes of total
nudity which could never have appeared in Spanish films until
after Franco's death, scenes that are quite torrid, erotic and
sensational even for Spanish audiences of the late 1970s.

The Spanish Civil War has always been a favorite theme
for Spanish directors and writers. In fact, Giménez-Rico
first thought of filming José María Gironella's spectacular
pentology about the Civil War beginning with The Cypresses
Believe in God, but felt it was too monumental a project. [5]
Giménez-Rico never has trouble with actors and chooses them
very carefully to be certain they represent the characters
they play to the best of their abilities. He never expected
Miguel Bose to turn in such a good performance since this
rock performer had to completely change his image and cut
his long hair. [6] Bose's voice was also dubbed because there
is too much of an Italian inflection in his Spanish pronunciation.

Family Portrait continues to be Giménez-Rico's best
film, for several reasons. Its story is sensitively mounted,
its production values are of a high caliber, the love story
and the outbursts of war and political violence are all extremely well handled, and the performances by all the actors
are superb. Giménez-Rico's next two films, Al fin, solos,
pero... (1977) and Del amor y la muerte (1978) were rather
prolix, banal films which were also unsuccessful commercially.
Upon leaving Madrid in 1982, the director had one project in
mind: Jarapelejos, based upon the novel of the same name by
the Generation of 1898 author Felipe Trigo, who committed
suicide in 1912. Giménez-Rico has much talent and one can
expect him to turn out another distinguished film in the realist tradition of Retrato de familia.

Two scenes from <u>Vestida de Azul</u> (Dressing in Blue, 1983). Above, José Antonio Sánchez; below, José Ruiz Orejon, Rene Amor, José Antonio Sánchez, Francisco Pérez de los Cabos, Juan Muñoz and Lorenzo Araña.

Most recently, Giménez-Rico carried forward his use
of realism when he filmed a documentary focusing on the
lives of six transvestites in Madrid, recording their fears,
passions and aspirations by means of a series of interviews
with them, their friends, and even their families. The subjects all work as male prostitutes and supplement their in-
comes in night clubs and shows. A fascinating documentary,
Vestida de azul (1983) contains some harrowing scenes, especially an operation on a man having a silicone "breast re-
pair." Many scenes among the transvestites are handled
delicately, others with broad vulgarity, indicating the new
sexual frankness and explicitness of Spanish cinema. Although the film is a bit repetitious and overlong, it is "not
a documentary in the classical sense, but a chatty, intimate
portrait of the transvestites' lives."[7] As part of the 1983
Festival of Spanish Films in New York, the film was greeted
with applause on opening night. Giménez-Rico is expert at
documentaries and traditional realist films. One wonders in
what direction he will move in the 1980s.

Bibliography

Besa, Peter. "Review of Retrato de familia." Variety
(Sept. 29, 1976), 30.

Besa, Peter. "Review of Vestida de azul." Variety (Oct.
12, 1983), 29.

Gonzáles, Miguel Angel. "Entrevista con A. Giménez-Rico."
Cinema 2002 No. 36 (Oct. 1976), 40-42.

Muñoz, Irene. "Review of Retrato de familia." Dirigido
por (Nov. 1976), 40.

Chapter 13

MANUEL GUTIERREZ ARAGON (1942)

Filmography

Short Films: 1969--El último día de la humanidad; 1970--
El Cordobés; 1979--Pruebas de niños (sketch for film Cuentos
para una escapada).

Feature Films: 1973--Habla, mudita (Speak, Dummy); 1977--
Camada negra (Black Brood); Sonámbulos (Sleepwalkers);
1978--El corazón del bosque (Heart of the Forest); 1979--
Maravillas (Marvels); 1982--Demonios en el jardín (Demons
in the Garden); 1983--Feroz; 1984--La noche más hermosa.

Born in 1942 in Torrelavega (Santander), Manuel Gutiérrez Aragón spent most of his youth and teenage years in
the country around Santander before coming to Madrid. Once
in the capital city, he took a degree in Liberal Arts, major-
ing in Philosophy at the University of Madrid, and later entered the National Film School where he majored in direction.

Photo above: Manuel Gutiérrez Aragón (Courtesy of the
Director).

He graduated in 1970, presenting his own film version of Hansel & Gretel for his final practicum.

Intellectually gifted, Gutiérrez is an excellent screenwriter, having collaborated on two of the most outstanding films made in Spain in 1976: Furtivos (Poachers), with José Luis Borau, and Las largas vacaciones del 36 (The Long Vacations of 1936), with Jaime Camino. Other earlier scripts include Corazón solitario (1972), with Francisco Betrui, and the following two with director José Luis García Sánchez: El lobo feroz (The Fercious Wolf, 1974) and Las truchas (The Trouts, 1977), which were both minor works.

Married and strictly dedicated to filmmaking after trying in 1979 to direct a theatrical revival of Kafka's The Trial (which proved disastrous). Gutiérrez has produced six feature films, all fascinating works on a variety of subjects. Considered by most film critics as one of the most stimulating and interesting filmmakers on the Spanish scene today, Gutiérrez deserves to be classified among the very best of those who are known internationally--Bardem, Berlanga, Buñuel and Saura. Like them, he is a "progressive director who executes his work with coherence and creativity, and is always concerned with maintaining and dispensing the bonds of communication with the spectator."[1]

Like Berlanga and Borau, Gutiérrez deserves an entire volume devoted to his work. It is difficult not to comment in detail upon each of his six feature films, since each opens new paths to his creativity and the communication between the filmmaker and his audience. In general, his principal preoccupation is the interplay of fantasy with reality. From this premise, it is possible to view the entire trajectory of his cinematic achievements.

Although at one time a student of José Luis Borau, whom Gutiérrez considers a realist director in the classic, lineal tradition, he calls himself a "baroque" director, and in this style, he searches for a more profound kind of cinema.[2] For Gutiérrez, the screenplay is everything--it must be in perfect order before filming begins. When the director talks of his "profound view of cinema," he is concerned particularly with "Spanish themes," themes that expose the people and the nation to broader intellectual vistas. This aesthetic, his baroque style coupled with a fervent Spanish nationalism, is Gutiérrez's modus operandi, evident in varying degrees in the productions he has filmed.

Angela Molina and José Luis López Vásquez in Habla, mudita (Speak, Dummy, 1973).

Habla, mudita (Speak, Dummy) is the director's first feature effort and should be viewed mostly as an apprentice work and not taken too seriously. Shot in color in and around Santander, it stars José Luis López Vásquez as a family man on vacation with his wife in Northern Spain. During their travels, he meets a young mute girl and begins to give her lessons and teach her to speak Spanish. In tackling this task he pits himself against centuries of ignorance and poverty. Making an enormous effort, he isolates himself from his own family and begins to live with the village mutes. Unlike François Truffaut's The Wild Child (which was a scientific exploration into the "civilizing" of a jungle boy, based upon historical fact), Habla, mudita is merely a trifle. López Vásquez, playing the role of Don Ramiro, a wealthy book publisher absorbed totally by the problems of language and communication, manages to teach the shepherd girl some vowel sounds and succeeds in teaching her words such as "bread" and "wheel." A relationship develops between the shepherdess and the publisher, but the latter's family, on learning that the two of them have run off together, believe the publisher has gone quite mad. The pair is discovered by a searching party of villagers, sleeping together in an old abandoned bus high in the mountains. Seeing the opportunity for some broad humor here, Gutiérrez has the villagers rock

the bus as the couple angrily storm out from their tryst.   Don
Ramiro, enraged because he is falsely accused of rape and
madness, begins to fight with the villagers.   Suddenly his
family arrives in their Mercedes-Benz with Madrid license
plates and they head back to the city.   The shepherdess runs
after the car and is left behind in the dust.   When she returns home, she begins to teach her "mute" brother the vowel
sounds.

Beautifully photographed by Luis Cuadrado and impec-
cably acted in superb rustic settings, Habla, mudita is Gutiérrez-Aragón's plea for enlightenment where ignorance exists.
Don Ramiro is a modern Don Quixote battling against the wind-
mills of big city conformity in his attempt to bring culture
and civilization to the villagers.   Though the intent of the
film is not always clear, Gutiérrez should be complimented
for breaking away from the conventional forms of film nar-
ration and telling a quite unconventional story about rustics
who are sometimes lovingly and sometimes bitterly characterized and caricatured in bizarre fashion.

Camada negra (Black Brood), filmed in 1977, eighteen
months after Franco's death, is "one of the most daring,
startling, outspoken and controversial films ever to be made
in Spain--a bombshell."[3]   Author Jorge Semprún said "a
democratic government, would, without doubt declare this film
of national interest and organize special sessions in schools,
colleges and universities for the foundation of its future citi-
zens."[4]   During the film's production, there were many attacks on bookstores and art galleries in Spain because of the
"fictional" events taking place in the film: the destruction of
bookstores, clandestine shootings, etc.   Black Brood is the
story of the "outlaw" political bands, anti-Falangist, anti-
regime, that arose after Franco's death.   Extremely well-
acted by a professional cast including Joaquín Hinojosa as
José, the leader of a young man's choir engaged in terrorist
activities, and María Luis Ponte as his mother Blanca, the
ideological force behind the group, the film focuses on José
Luis Alonso (Tatín), her teenage son who seeks to enter the
group.   She indoctrinates her sons into the choir's concept of
heroism: keep a secret, avenge insults to a comrade and be
ready to sacrifice one's nearest and dearest for the cause of
the group.   The fifteen-year-old boy secretly resolves to fulfill all these conditions.   He assaults a girl who has insulted
one of his brothers.   While trying to rape her, he is caught
by a young waitress (played by Angela Molina) with whom he
shares a tragic love affair.   Molina plays Rosa, a naive,
warm-hearted girl, giving, tender, muddling along in a world

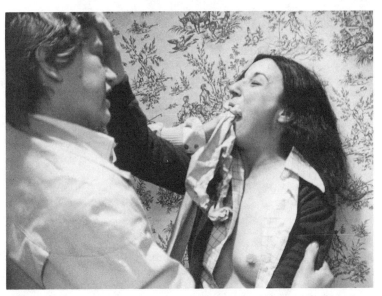

Two scenes from Gutiérrez Aragón's Camada negra (Black Brood, 1977). Top, José Luis Alonso; below, Alonso fighting with Angela Molina.

she barely understands with her illegitimate child. Tatín becomes her protector, but in his desire to become a good
Fascist-terrorist, he kills her, in one of the most shockingly
brutal and cruel scenes ever filmed. He makes love to her
and while she is in the throes of her passion, bashes her
head in repeatedly with a stone, shouting "For Spain! For
Spain! For Spain!" He then hides the body in a hole, one
of a number dug for saplings which are being planted in a
nearby forest. With this last act of extreme cruelty, Tatín
has come of age and is officially inducted into the choral
(terrorist) group. The film ends as Rosa's baby boy searches
aimlessly for his mother, only to become lost and probably
die in the forest.

  Black Brood is a direct attack on the Franco establish-
ment, and more than just a political thriller made in the style
of Costa-Gavras. Gutiérrez said that with this film he tried
to demonstrate "the fascism latent in so many situations in
our lives."[5] At the film's conclusion, any hero can objec-
tively be a right-wing Fascist. "But the most heroic hero
is the one who fights against something he cannot change,
such as history, because that is the most irrational fight that
exists."[6]

  Sonámbulos (Somnambulists) is one of Gutiérrez-Aragón's
most stylistically "baroque" films, and quite mystifying. It
is a difficult film to "read" (analyze) because there are so
many elements in the plot that appear understated, discon-
nected, confused, hermetic, unreal, surreal, mystical, mythic,
laden with symbols that are never fully explained. Brilliant
on its own terms, it is directed chiefly towards an intellectual,
elitist audience. Where Black Brood was a linear, compre-
hensible, straightforward, hardhitting tale, Somnambulists is
exactly the reverse.

  Set in Madrid in 1960, it stars Ana Belén as Ana, a
woman acting as a revolutionary for a secret society. She
is first beaten and then condemned to death by a military
court. She collapses, suffers epileptic fits and is taken home
by her uncle, Norman, a doctor (played by Norman Briski)
who can no longer practice because he was caught by the
police for smuggling pharmaceuticals. Lola Gaos plays a
maid named Fatima who works for Ana and can sometimes
cure her because she wears the amulet of a rooster's claw
upon her chest, which gives her magical powers. Her efforts
to heal Ana fail and the latter winds up in a sanatorium where
every "patient" appears "crazy." Ana's son Andresito reads
to her from a mysterious book--an allegory about a queen, a

magician, a mortally wounded princess, a book with "marvels" that contains some hidden meaning. Apparently, Ana's problem is that she finds the key to the "book of marvels"; it turns out to be a key to a closet door behind which her father and mother are working for a clandestine Communist or feminist or fascist cell. Ana takes the magician's advice and reports her mother (the queen) to the police. The Civil Guards, however, consider Ana's tale hysterical and unbalanced, and she is subsequently returned to the sanatorium. Sonámbulos ends with some wonderfully mystifying statements; for example, "You can never have all the questions or all the answers to anything and should never ask all the questions or look for all the answers."

There is one thrilling surrealist scene in Sonámbulos when mounted police crash through the huge windows of a library, routing protesters. It is reminiscent of a similar scene in Ivan Passer's American film, Cutter's Way, when John Heard rides on horseback into the living room of a Long Island mansion. The photography by Teo Escamilla and the sets are also conceived brilliantly, sustaining the unique mood of this film.

Sonámbulos resists interpretation or decoding. It is an extremely difficult film about the constant struggle to acquire knowledge--knowledge of the nature of things and events, of intimate and group motivations. It is complex, elaborate, literate, visually and scenically splendid, but it is also obscure, unnerving, unconventional, irrational, and a change of direction for this director.

El corazón del bosque (Heart of the Forest) returns Gutiérrez Aragón and his audience to familiar turf--the forests of Cantabria and Asturias where the director spent his youth. Set in 1952, it stars Luis Politti as El Andarín, a Basque revolutionary, a separatist who refuses to surrender to the Nationalist government, and Norman Briski as Juan, who searches for El Andarín throughout the entire film. Angela Molina plays Amparo, in love with the noble guerrilla although now engaged to the local shoemaker. When her brother Juan returns to Cantabria, she discourages his search for El Andarín. Juan refuses and Amparo frustrates Juan's search by hiding El Andarín in a local cornfield. Briski finally catches up with the anarchist, but is mistakenly taken for El Andarín and almost shot to death by the local Civil Guards. El Andarín saves Briski, but Briski shoots him because he mistakenly believes El Andarín has betrayed their separatist movement. Amparo and her new husband offer Briski shelter,

but the Civil Guard now comes looking for him. As El
Andarín prophesied, "You cannot trust anybody!" Briski takes
over the role of El Andarín, becoming an "animal" in the
forest, surrounded by the Civil Guard, continually on the run,
living off the earth to survive.

The real star of this film is the countryside of Asturias.
The mist is everywhere. It rolls in magically and endows
the struggle of the hunter and the hunted with great natural
beauty. Although the struggle to survive is the film's major
theme, love and its betrayal are also important thematic con-
siderations. Unlike Sonámbulos, in this film the story is told
simply, straightforwardly, without artifice, but with much
artistic feeling for the countryside and its people. El corazón
del bosque is a very sensual film, full of atmosphere, glori-
fying the geographical beauties of Northern Spain. Apparently
it is based upon a real event of the 1930s when the Maquís
had offered armed resistance to the Franco government, and
a few "outlaws," hiding themselves in the mountains, became
mythical figures. Gutiérrez has taken some of these childhood myths he grew up with and, as he does not in his ex-
periments with baroque style, filmed this story in a terse,
sober manner, corroborating his "traditional" training as a
realist filmmaker.

Always seeking some new subject, Gutiérrez returns
in Maravillas to baroque stylistics aided by many exotic elements. One of the biggest problems with this film is the
wavering plot. Maravillas is the name of a teenage girl of
fifteen who lives with her wayward father (played by Fernando
Fernán Gómez), an unemployed photographer who likes to
steal money from his daughter for his erotic vices which he
pursues in a local massage parlor. María Maravillas is
growing up. The film shows her sexual initiation and her
constant need to spend money. Since her father steals from
her, she seeks out her "godfathers"--all Sephardic Jews who
spoil her, especially Uncle Solomon. But the latter was forbidden to see Maravillas again after he subjected her to a
"test"--making her walk along the top of a high wall, risking
death so that she would no longer be afraid in life.

As Maravillas grows older, she meets a boy who works
with Solomon, another magician and entertainer. The boy
plays the role of Caryl Chessman, the convicted murderer
doomed to die in the electric chair. (The boy learns to free
himself by magic from the chair, one of the show's spectacular routines.) Maravillas becomes involved with him in a
jewel robbery. When they take an emerald to a fence, the
latter is mysteriously strangled and the emerald disappears.

Gutiérrez Aragón's <u>Maravillas</u> (<u>Marvels</u>, 1979). Top, Cristina Marcos; below, Fernando Fernán Gómez with Marcos.

Because of his dissolute living and constant need for cash, Maravilla's father becomes the main suspect in the crime. However, Solomon, at the banquet of Maravillas' "godfathers," forces the boy, "Chessman," to confess that it was he who stole the emerald and murdered the fence. Maravillas is saved once again by her family, but at the cost of losing her first lover.

The film's images are startlingly beautiful at times and the Madrid location is used to fine advantage. All the actors, especially Cristina Marcos (Maravillas), Fernando Fernán Gómez (her father), Enrique Sanfrancisco ("Chessman") and Francisco Merino (Solomon), are especially fine. Gutiérrez Aragón uses some interesting film techniques, fading to red instead of to black when a scene ends; he also cleverly superimposes one image over another, one face upon another as he bridges between scenes. His use of ancient chants and Sephardic music is also thrilling and original. There is a great feeling for the sensuality inherent in the Sephardic lifestyle, the attention paid to the erotic and the sexual. For all this, Maravillas as a film remains a curiously hermetic, inpenetrable work, once again appealing to a very limited audience. Gutiérrez seems to waver between the extremes of linear traditional filmmaking and experimentally baroque works. Maravillas as a film works on many levels, projecting intense feelings for teenagers in love, for the relationship between fathers and daughters, between grandparents and grandchildren. One critic said, "When this film ends, you have to rub your eyes. You have seen a circus that discovers painful, hidden aspects, painful intuitions of reality.... Maravillas is committed to liberty, disassembles accepted wisdom, does not offer moralizing, does not offer good intentions; it offers art."[7]

Gutiérrez Aragón's last film which I saw in Spain in a rough-cut the summer of 1982, finally opened in New York City in March of 1984. Demonios en el jardín (Demons in the Garden), a return to traditional filmmaking, is an atmospheric film set in the early 1940s. Produced by the very talented Luis Megino, Demons is the story of a family and its seething sexuality, jealousies, dreams realized and shattered, hypocrisies. It stars Angela Molina and Ana Belén as the lovers of Juan (played by Imanol Arias) and Oscar (Eusebio Lázaro), and the screenplay deals with a mother's devotion (Gloria, the mother, is played by Encarna Paso) for her two sons. The brothers, Juan and Oscar, have frequent violent disputes. Juan leaves the family store, called "El Jardín" and run by his mother, and joins the Nationalist Army. Oscar and Ana

Alvaro Sánchez-Prieto and Angela Molina in <u>Demonios en el jardín</u> (<u>Demons in the Garden,</u> 1982).

marry but remain childless, and Angela is left pregnant by
Juan. She gives birth to Juanito and he becomes ill while
searching for his father as the years pass by. Gloria takes
Juanito into her store and pampers the boy, who is, incidentally, her only heir. Juanito, however, misses his mother
and she returns to live with the family, within El Jardín.
One day, Juanito hears that his father will pass with Franco's
retinue; he finally meets him and discovers that he is only a
waiter in the service of Franco's personal bodyguard. The
years move on and Juanito, no longer suffering from a rheu-
matic heart condition and totally disenchanted with his father,
learns that his father is visiting Ana, Oscar's wife. Apparently, Ana and Juan had been lovers many years before. Because Juan now needs money, Ana steals one thousand pesetas
from the safe. Juan has been cashiered out of the army and
has run up many debts. Gloria, Juan's mother, discovers
the theft but blames it upon Angela, who is dragged off to
jail by the local Civil Guards. Gloria discovers the truth
and urges Juan to return home to marry Angela so that the
family will have a "legitimate" heir. Angela, however, refuses to marry the callow Juan, who is still in love with Ana.

Returning once again to El Jardín, Juan again tries
to seduce Ana, but she is so enraged by Juan's behavior that
she shoots him in the shoulder with a hand gun. Oscar and

Juan fight fiercely in their own love-hate relationship, first over Ana, then Angela. On the following day, Juanito's birthday is celebrated and the entire family is gathered by the local photographer for a family portrait in front of "El Jardín". The film ends in a "freeze-frame" of the photograph, offering no conclusions, but exposing all the hidden hypocrisies within this petit-bourgeois family.

Demonios en el jardín contains one lovely, nostalgic scene, when Juanito goes to a local movie house and watches Silvana Mangano do the mambo number from the Italian classic Anna, indicating his own sexual stirrings and worries. Demons burns with a certain intensity and Gutiérrez Aragón here begins to achieve the prominence of a Buñuel or a Saura. Archer Winston "places this film among the very greatest to have come out of Spain. It does, indeed, blaze with quiet, demonic power."[8] Demonios is Gutiérrez Aragón's best film to date. He has demonstrated the courage to develop scenarios oriented towards more intellectually-inclined cinema audiences, but his real forte is undoubtedly the traditional realist films he directs so beautifully. Demonios en el jardin is the best example of this kind of film. It will be interesting to see in which direction Gutiérrez moves in the 1980s.

Bibliography

Book G. Aragón, M. & Megino, L. Maravillas (Madrid: Ed. JC, 1981), 125 pages.

Articles

Antolín, M. "Review of Sonámbulos." Cinema 2002 (June 1978), 46-48.

Antolín, M. "Review of Corazón del bosque." Cinema 2002 (Feb. 1979), 38-41.

Besa, Peter. "Review of Camada negra." Variety (May 11, 1977), 79, 95.

Besa, Peter. "Review of Sonámbulos." Variety (Oct. 18, 1978), 18.

Besa, Peter. "Review of Demonios en el jardín." Variety (Oct 6, 1982), 16.

Besa, Peter. "Review of Feroz." Variety (May 2, 1984), 18.

Besa, Peter. "Review of La noche más hermosa (The Most Beautiful Night)." Variety (Oct. 10, 1984), 20.

Boyero, Carlos. "Review of Maravillas." Casablanca (Mar. 1981), 41-42.

Castro, Antonio. "Entrevista con M.G. Aragón." Dirigido por No. 48, pp. 20-29.

Castro, Antonio. "Entrevista con M.G. Aragón." Dirigido por No. 72, pp. 48-56.

Freixas, Ramón. "M.G. Aragón: Las maravillas del bosque." Dirigido por No. 82, pp. 44-53.

Hawk. "Review of Habla, mudita." Variety (July 4, 1973), 18.

González, M.A. "Review of Camada negra." Cinema 2002 (Sept. 1977), 46-48.

Mosk. "Review of El corazón del bosque." Variety (Mar. 21, 1979), 24.

Mosk. "Review of Maravillas." Variety (Mar. 11, 1981), 26.

"Entrevistas con M.G. Aragón." Fotogramas (Jul-Aug. 1982), 13-16.

"El último rodaje de M. Gutiérrez." Fotogramas (Jul-Aug. 1982), 17-18.

"M.G. Aragón." Contracampo (Dec. 1979), 21-36.

"M.G. Aragón." Contracampo (Mar. 1981), 3-5.

Winsten, Archer. "Spanish 'Demons' Burns with Intensity." New York Post (Mar. 2, 1984), 53.

General Article

Clarens, Carlos. "Is There Film After Buñuel?" Village Voice (Jan. 17, 1984), 45-46. Contains a review of Demonios en el jardín.

Chapter 14

PILAR MIRO (1940)

Filmography

1976--La petición; 1978--Sábado de gloria; 1979-80--El crimen de Cuenca (The Crime of Cuenca); 1981--Gary Cooper, que estás en los cielos (Gary Cooper, Thou That Art in Heaven); 1982--Hablamos esta noche (We'll Talk Tonight).

Of the few women directing films today in Spain, Pilar Miró is certainly the most outstanding. A native of Madrid, she was born there on April 20, 1940. Having studied both Law and Journalism at the university, she also took a degree in Screenwriting at the Official Film School (Escuela Oficial de Cinema). She then began working in Spanish television in 1960, first for the publicity department, and then in 1966 she began directing for television. Her first program for TV was a drama called Lilí; since then she has worked periodically for Spanish television. Some of her prize-winning TV programs are Una fecha señalada, Hora once, Estudio 1, Novela, Danza macabra (Strindberg), and El escarabajo de oro (Poe). In 1964, she co-scripted El juego de la oca, directed by Manuel Summers. Her own career as a director began twelve years later with her first film, La petición (The Engagement Party), starring Ana Belén and based upon a novel by Emile Zola. It immediately demonstrated Miró's considerable directorial talent. According to the film critic Vincent Molina-Foix, "La petición deeply shocked the Spanish censors who, in the relatively liberal times following Franco's death, banned it totally."[1] Apparently released after some fellow directors and the press brought pressure to bear upon the government, La petición is like a television film, "the gruesome story of a beautiful and wealthy young girl, simultaneously involved in sadistic and ultimately fatal sexual relationships with three men."[2]

Ana Belén in Pilar Miró's La petición (The Engagement Party, 1976).

      Although her next film, Sábado de gloria (1978), re-
ceived very little critical attention, Pilar Miró's career cata-
pulted to international attention when El crimen de Cuenca
(The Crime of Cuenca) was released in 1980. Miró warned
me about seeing Cuenca in local theaters in Madrid; she was
worried that bombs might be set off in an attempt to prevent
the public from seeing the film's starkly realistic depiction
of police brutality. [3] The film was confiscated by a military
court, which also attempted to try her because Cuenca revealed illegal methods of interrogation by the police under
the Franco regime, now strongly prohibited by the present
Constitution. In a typical and contradictory move, "on March
30, 1981, the military embargo on the film El crimen de
Cuenda, first imposed in 1979, was lifted and the case against
its director, Pilar Miró, withdrawn."[4] The year 1981, however will go down as a record for Cuenca, as one of the
greatest money-making films in Spanish history. "According
to official sources, it was seen by 1,972,000 people, the over-
all box-office take amounting to 370 million pesetas (about
$4 million)."[5] Because the film was banned for so many
years and as a result of the threat of military proceedings

against Miró, Cuenca turned out to be Spain's box-office champion.

Gary Cooper, que estás en los cielos was made directly after Cuenca and was released in Madrid in 1982. The film was shown in the United States in December 1982 as part of a series of lectures and films on the theme of "The Spanish Woman Today," presented by the Spanish Institute and the Center for American-Spanish Affairs. Pilar Miró came to New York City to lecture on this film and discussed her role as a woman director in the Spanish art world. When I met Pilar Miró earlier at a lecture at the Cine Club Alphaville, she told me she was filming Hablamos esta noche (We'll Talk About It Tonight), with Mercedes Sampietro and Victor Valverde of Gary Cooper. It deals with the extra-marital

Victor Valverde and Daniel Dicenta in Hablamos esta noche (1982).

affairs and divorce of a young Spanish couple, formerly another taboo subject for Spanish directors. Although Hablamos esta noche has not been seen internationally (except at the Montreal Film Festival in Canada in 1983), its story about the crisis in the life of a nuclear engineer who breaks with his female partner, finds a new woman and lives through an ethical and professional conflict is based upon some of Miró's own personal experiences, although, like Gary Cooper, the film is not autobiographical.

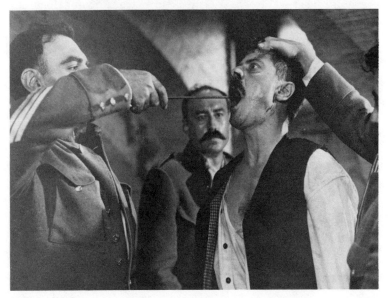

Two scenes from Pilar Miró's <u>El crimen de Cuenca</u> (1980).
Above, Fernando Rey (c.) and Héctor Alterio; below, Francisco
Casares and Daniel Dicenta.

The controversy surrounding the career of Pilar Miró
stems from the motivations behind her films. Unlike her
contemporary, Josefina Molina, Miró is a very dynamic personality. Unmarried and independent, she is trying to re-
educate the modern Spanish woman by posing and exposing
their problems as the raw material of a new type of cinema
that may be loosely referred to as "feminist cinema." Although her early films show women constantly exploited in a
male-chauvinist, macho-oriented society, her last two prose-
lytize for feminine independence and interdependence with men,
and the opportunity for all women to lead productive lives.

El crimen de Cuenca deals with the realistic portrayal
of an historical event. It is a wonderfully evocative, realistically detailed film shot in color in the actual locales where
the "supposed" crime took place. It is about Gregorio (Daniel
Dicenta) and Juan (José Manuel Cervino) who are accused of
killing a fellow shepherd named Cepa, who disappeared from
their town in and around Castile in the early 1900s. Charges
are trumped up and brought against these men by a local
right-wing congressman, Contreras (Fernando Rey), and an
ambitious judge, Isasa (Hector Alterio). These two civil
servants ordered the Civil Guards to extract confessions and
determine what the peasants did with the shepherd's body
after they had supposedly robbed him. The peasants are
brutally tortured. There are about fifteen to twenty minutes'
worth of torture scenes in the film that portray graphically
the police methods of the Guardia Civil during the early 1900s.
Both men are forced to confess to the crime and are brought
to trial. They plead guilty, serve six years of fifteen-year
sentences, and are given probation for good behavior. Two
years later, the supposed victim of their crime returns to
Cuenca. The two peasants, Gregorio and León, who have
lived through torture, self-hate, self-torment and hatred of
each other, finally embrace in the last minutes of the film.
The men are finally vindicated by the same congressman and
judge who originally fomented the trial and wanted to see
"justice" done at the expense of the real truth. Pilar Miró
has taken a documented story and portrayed graphically and
realistically the political, emotional and social behavior of
the protagonists of the period. The film is a plea to end
police brutality, political subversion and provincial ignorance
in Cuenca and throughout Spain.

Miró's efforts to emancipate Spanish women came to
the fore in her next film, Gary Cooper, que estás en los
cielos (1981). The film covers three days in the life of Andrea (Mercedes Sampietro). Andrea is a television director

Mercedes Sampietro and Jon Finch in <u>Gary Cooper, que</u>
<u>estás en los cielos</u> (1981).

in her early thirties. She is in love with Mario, a fellow
journalist played by Jon Finch, and she is pregnant. However, Mario does not want Andrea to have their child. Although Mario and Andrea live together, he has just begun a
new affair with a photographer. Andrea is left virtually alone
to cope with her problem. She sees her doctor and is told
she must check into a local clinic immediately and undergo
an abortion because he has discovered cancerous tumors.
Stunned by the news, Andrea takes stock of her life. With
her, we enter the world of a woman as television director.
As she begins to shoot a TV film, her behavior toward the
actors changes. She is suddenly offered a job directing a
motion picture but declines, not telling her producer the real
reason for her refusal. She tries to confide in Mario the
reasons for her "abortion," but he disclaims all responsibility
for her decision. When Andrea discovers Mario's affair with
his photographer, her world begins to fall apart. She visits
her mother, picks up some old love letters and movie star
photos, especially one of Gary Cooper; she even prays to
him (in a voice-over), parodying the Lord's Prayer, asking
Gary for help. (She is, after all, a woman living in the
world of film, her only reality.) Andrea, in several emotional scenes, begins to sort out her life: she leaves her
apartment in order and makes a cassette and sends it with a
letter to her first lover, Bernardo (Fernando Delgado). Bernardo listens to the cassette and arrives at the clinic just

before Andrea is wheeled into the operating room. At this
point, the end titles would have been appropriate. But Miró
insists on taking us into the operating room with Andrea.
The surgeon asks her to relax, have confidence. She takes
his hand--and voilá, the expected freeze-frame of clasping
hands. We never know Andrea's fate at the hands of the
surgeon.

Gary Cooper is a film in which we share the heroine's
frustrations. For the first time (in Spanish cinema) we are
privileged to enter into the intimate thoughts of a professional
woman, her problems, her feelings, fears, joys, betrayals,
trepidation. Will there be a tomorrow? At one point, Andrea
has a brief affair with a friend's husband because she wants
to feel the warmth and contact of a human being able to understand her and her problems, although she never really con-
fides in her lover. An inconsequential visit by a plumber as
she is about to leave her apartment for the clinic is a very
touching scene because of Andrea's yearning for humanity
and a little sympathy, even from a stranger. Even Andrea's
mother, involved with her own problems, gives her daughter
very little time. When Andrea asks her, "What would you
do if I were to die tomorrow? What are the last things you
would say to me?" Her mother thinks for a moment and
answers, "Andrea, I'm in a hurry. I have to go." Miró
captures the essence of the lack of relationship between mother
and daughter, as well as the lack of communication between
Andrea and Mario in a modern urban setting. Gary Cooper
is a bravura film, sensitively written and directed. It is
very similar to Agnes Varda's Cléo de 5 à 7 (Cleo from 5 to
7), which starred Corinne Marchand as a Parisian woman
with whom we share two difficult hours of joy and sorrow,
but Miró's film is vastly superior. Gary Cooper is a very
personal film, introspective and upbeat. Although we never
know if her surgery is successful, we are left feeling that
Andrea has matured and can face the future.

Apparently, Miró herself had undergone an open heart
operation which she came through successfully. [6] Like Andrea,
too, she had undergone some self-analysis, gauging her successes and failures. Although one may consider this film
semi-autobiographical, Miró's recent successes all exhibit a
pro-feminist ideology and a constant search for independence
and future happiness. If she continues in the autobiographical
vein, one hopes that her future personal experiences will be
less tinged with the near maudlin or lachrymose and that the
vigor of her strong personality (her "masculine" side as evidenced in her capable handling of the strong themes of El

crimen de Cuenca) will take root and prosper in the actresses who represent her alter ego. Miró is an enigma. Perhaps her role as director is in flux, like that of the Spanish career woman of the 1980s. Miró displays both an extremely sensitive feminism and a forceful masculinity in her films and in real life, and a personality that is tempered by an eloquent grace and refinement, peculiarly and particularly Spanish. Her past films and her future ones will always command our interest.

Late in 1983, Miró's career had taken a new turn. Appointed the new Director General of Cinema by the Spanish Government, Miró presides over various boards dealing with all phases of the Spanish film industry. Her most recent controversial act was to create a new series of "classifications" of films based on the age of audiences. Her leadership in this new reclassification system is coming under attack as well as her "moral capacities,"[7] Once again, Miró is at the forefront of another controversial issue in the Spanish film industry. One hopes that her entry into the politics of cinema will not detract from her career as one of Spain's leading feminist directors.

Bibliography

Besa, Peter. "Review of La petición." Variety (Aug. 25, 1976), 20.

Besa, Peter. "Review of El crimen de Cuenca." Variety (Jan. 23, 1980), 104.

Besa, Peter. "Review of Gary Cooper, Who Art in Heaven." Variety (Feb. 4, 1981), 20.

Besa, Peter. "Review of Hablamos esta noche." Variety (Sept. 1, 1982), 19.

Castro, Antonio. "Entrevista con Pilar Miró." Dirigido por No. 71, 4-7, 34-38.

Freixas, Ramón. "Review of Gary Cooper..." Dirigido por No. 79, 61-62.

Hernández-Les, J. "P. Miró: La cineasta de la crueldad." Fotogramas (July 1981), 33-36.

Hernández-Les, J. "Buscando mi camino." Casablanca (May 1982), 9-10.

Marinero, Pachín. "Review of El crimen de Cuenca." Casablanca (Sept. 1981), 55.

Markham, James M. "Spanish Regime in First Film Ban." New York Times (Jan. 6, 1980), C 6.

"P. Miró Indicted; Pic 'Insult' Alleged." Variety (Apr. 23, 1980), 1.

Chapter 15

PEDRO OLEA (1938)

Filmography

Short films: 1962--Ultima página; 1963--Parque de juegos; 1964--Anábel; Ceremonia secreta.

Feature Films: 1967--Días de viejo color; 1968--Juan y Junior en un mundo diferente; 1970--El bosque de lobos (The Wolf Forest); 1971--La casa sin fronteras; 1973--No es bueno que el hombre esté solo; 1974--Tormento (Torment); 1975--Pim, pam, pum... ¡fuego!; 1976--La Corea; 1977--Un hombre llamado 'Flor de otoño' (A Man Called 'Autumn Flower'); 1984--Akelarre (Witches' Sabbath).

Pedro Olea was born in Bilbao in 1938 and began his studies in Economics before coming to Madrid in the early

Above, Pedro Olea in 1977 (photo courtesy of the director).

1960s. He loved to play hooky from school and see the big Hollywood production films he still admires so much today.[1] Extremely dissatisfied with his choice of career (he never finished his degree in Economics), he entered the National Film School (E. O. C.) and graduated in 1964. He made four short films there: Ultima página dealt with a woman who commits suicide; Parque de juegos was a science fiction story by Ray Bradbury; Anábel was based upon a story by Marco Denevi, and Secret Ceremony is another Denevi tale that fascinated Olea as a student. Upon graduation, he went directly to work for Spanish television, began writing film criticism for Nuestro cine, a leading magazine, and also worked in publicity.

His first feature film, Días de viejo color (1967), was an amateur effort. It dealt with a group of Madrillian college students who spend their Easter vacation on the Costa del Sol and the events that occur there, very much like a Spanish version of M-G-M's Where the Boys Are! Olea believes that his first really important film was El bosque de lobos (The Wolf Forest), with José Luis López Vásquez. He still considers it his favorite among all his films,[2] and López Vásquez the single actor he most enjoyed working with.

Pedro Olea chats with Geraldine Chaplin on the set of La casa sin fronteras (1971).

Returning to the Basque country, Olea made La casa sin fronteras (1971), a suspense film starring Tony Isbert and Geraldine Chaplin. House Without Boundaries is a "tale of innocence meshed within a web of evil. Olea's aim is not to shock, but to reveal the inexorable workings of an all-powerful organization stamped with all the signs of a corrupt, sadistic, self-righteous secret order."[3] Olea shot this film in his hometown of Bilbao and by a remote Basque fishing village, but the real locale is the home town of anyone threatened by self-appointed societies and secret organizations. Olea had little difficulty working with international players such as Viveca Lindfors, Geraldine Chaplin and Patty Shepard. He left the identity of the secret organization rather vague so as not to encourage the wrath of the curious, but Casa sin fronteras was seen by many as an allegory of the powerful, politico-religious society Opus Dei. Although the film had little success in Spain, it was a nominee for an Academy Award in the Best Foreign Film category.

Intending to film Leopoldo Alas' well-known novel La Regenta, Olea had to content himself with filming No es bueno el hombre que esté solo (It's Not Good for a Man to Be Alone). It was a box office success in Spain in 1972 but most critics outside the nation considered it plainly awful. Similar to

J. L. López Vásquez and unidentified actress in Olea's No es bueno que el hombre esté solo (1973).

Berlanga's Life-Size, it is the story of a man who treats a
"doll" as if it were a woman of flesh and blood. The film
could have explored the themes of one man's loneliness, but
it became a commercial success because it dealt with the
"pathological" aspects of the problem, not the psychological
or sociological ones.

Tormento (Torment, 1974), based upon the famous
novel by Pérez Galdós, is Olea's best film to date. Filmed
in color and starring Ana Belén and Francisco Rabal, it was
Olea's biggest commercial success. Olea considers himself
a practitioner of realist cinema who specializes in period
dramas. He enjoys making costume dramas more than any
other type of film.[4] His next two films, Pim, pam, pum,
... ¡fuego! (1975) and La Corea (1976) are "modern" works
that suffer from poor screenplays, poor dialogue, and censorship due to off-color themes and dialogues. Olea, however, is an excellent technician. All his films have a very
expert look. He admits that Bertolucci and Hitchcock have
greatly influenced his work.[5]

His most recent film, Un hombre llamado 'Flor de
otoño' (A Man Called 'Autumn Flower', 1978) seems to have
brought Olea both the professional and the commercial success
which had eluded this talented filmmaker to this point in his
career. He is constantly searching for his own vision, his
personal style. His strengths lie in recapturing on film the
myths of the Basque country, recreating the drama of well-
known nineteenth-century novels and making heavily-laden
costume dramas that deal with the Spanish Civil War and the
period after. A discussion of his best three films will illus-
trate these polarities in his multifaceted career.

El bosque de lobos (The Wolf Forest, 1974), Olea's
Gothic film, had its origins in "Anábel," a story by Mario
Denevi upon which the American film director, Joseph Losey,
based his film Secret Ceremony. Its subject, essentially, is
lycanthropy and it is set in the eerie, northern landscapes
of Galicia (Pontevedra) in the late nineteenth century; José
Luis López Vásquez plays the role of a werewolf. Apparently
stunned as a child while watching horses play sexually, López
Vásquez becomes a "wolf man" of sorts. He has a serious
appetite for women and shocks, bites, violates, and then
kills them. Lobos is a gory but captivating film which begins
as a character study of a lone peddler but becomes a detective
story when articles of apparel disappear from the dead women
and reappear as gifts from the peddler to other women, who
soon disappear mysteriously themselves. The "wolf man" is

Scene from Olea's El bosque de lobos (1974), with José Luis López Vásquez.

ensnared in the forest by a bear trap and the local priest and villagers set out to kill him; however, they later set him free and make him stand trial for murder. Olea's third film, El bosque de lobos is a work of maturity and is full of images of plastic beauty. López Vásquez gives an extremely intelligent and dramatic performance and it is a pity that the film has never been seen internationally. Because Olea was dissatisfied with his first two films, Lobos became a cooperative film effort of several young filmmakers, which was in direct contradiction to Olea's own past studies and training. Nevertheless, Lobos is a moving story whose essential theme is a plea for understanding in the face of poverty, superstition and magic. It offers no conclusions concerning the origins of wolf-men but presents its myth with dignity and humanity.

Tormento (1974) reveals Olea's talent at adapting great nineteenth-century Spanish novels, reconstructing in minute detail the social and political backgrounds against which the protagonists move in his scenario. It is an extraordinarily beautiful film to look at, "limned with good taste which

Francisco Rabal and Ana Bélen in Olea's <u>Torment</u> (1974).

beautifully captures the chapters of Galdós and expertly probes into the lives and problems" of the characters. [6]

Tormento stars Ana Belén as Amparo, a pretty servant girl, and Francisco Rabal as an indiano (a Spaniard who struck it rich in the New World) who returns to visit his relatives in Spain and is also looking for a wife. At his cousin's home he meets Amparo, who is having an amorous but inconclusive affair with a "wavering" priest. The latter's family wants him to end his sexual relationship with her, but he threatens suicide. Amparo meanwhile, is impressed by the attentions paid to her by Pedro (Francisco Rabal), who is also deeply in love with her. Never admitting Amparo's liaison with the priest to Pedro himself, the priest's mother informs on the affair to Pedro's cousin. When Pedro reveals that he knows about Amparo's affair she takes an overdose of laudanum. At first it seems she will die, but later we find that she is on the road to recovery. As Pedro says goodbye to her before returning to Latin America, Olea cuts his next scene to the train station. Pedro's family, who have always profited from his generosity, are all bidding him farewell as he shouts through the train's compartment window, "I guess I'll never marry anyone." Amparo, seated next to Pedro, comes to the compartment window and waves to the family as the train slowly chugs out of the station. Pedro's cousin repeats under her breath, "¡Puta! ¡Puta! ¡Puta!" (Whore, whore, whore!).

Galdós' philosophy comes through at the end of the film. Pedro is the incarnation of Galdós' vision--that truth, not hypocrisy, love, not hate are the real codes to live by in the modern world. Laws should be tempered with humanity. One should not live according to societal conventions alone or according to the superficial codes of an aristocratic society. Pedro represents the new American spirit of freedom which is totally unacceptable in the decadent society of late nineteenth-century Madrid.

Tormento boasts excellent performances by all performers. Francisco Rabal is especially fine as Pedro, but Ana Belén steals the film from him as Amparo, displaying a cool charm that masks her burning sexuality. Javier Escriva as the tormented priest delivers a splendid but thankless performance. Only Conchita Velasco, as the vicious, gossipy cousin who seeks to destroy Pedro's love affair for her own selfish motives and financial gain, rivals Belen's performance. Although there is nothing new to be seen in Tormento, Olea has very capably re-told Galdós' story with

Francisco Rabal (1.), Ana Bélen and Concha Velasco (c.) in Olea's Torment (1974).

fine production values in the fashion of traditional realist cinema. Tormento was seen in the United States as part of the American Film Institute's New Spanish Cinema Series in 1979-80.

In 1975, Pim, pam, pum,... ¡fuego! (1, 2, 3, Fire! or Bang, Bang! You're Dead) did not catch fire internationally, despite its title, probably because its treatment of post-war music hall life in Spain was a very, very limited subject. It featured, however, excellent performances by Fernando Fernán Gómez and Conchita Velasco. It was last seen in the 1983 Spanish Film Festival in New York at the Guild Theatre with thirteen other features and surprisingly etched an indelible portrait of Madrid of the 1940s. It is the old, old story of a young woman in love with two men: a young revolutionary she saves from death and an older man who murders her out of jealousy of her idyllic love for a younger man.

La Corea (1976) was also seen as pallid by the critics. It dealt with the sexual propinquities of an older woman and a young boy. Here is further evidence of the "new freedom"

Concha Velasco in a scene from Pim, pam, pum... ¡fuego!
(1975).

in Spanish cinema to portray such themes on the screen, but Olea does it with much too little psychological penetration or comprehension of the motives of its leading characters.

Un hombre llamado 'Flor de otoño' (A Man Called 'Autumn Flower') sums up the best and worst qualities of Pedro Olea's somewhat erratic directorial career. Filmed in color and set in the 1930s, it was made in and around Barcelona in 1977. Flor de otoño is the story of a wealthy aristocratic lawyer, Lluís de Serracant (played expertly by José Sacristán), who belongs to an illustrious Catalonian family. Lluís apparently leads a normal professional life by day, but by night he becomes "Flor de otoño" ("Autumn Flower"), a transvestite homosexual performer in a low local cabaret. His lover, a

Scene from Un hombre llamado 'Flor de otoño' (1977), with José Sacristán on lap of Roberto Camarchel.

combination boxer-bodyguard, protects Lluis in his dangerous
double life. The screenplay has many plot twists. Lluis is
always fearful that his homosexuality will be discovered by
his illustrious family, especially his mother. As a transvestite performer, he becomes involved in many sordid situations, including the murder of a fellow performer with whom
he had argued the previous night. Believing that Lluis murdered his lover, Armengol, a drug pusher, kidnaps him, beats
him brutally and dumps him, dressed "in drag," on his
mother's doorstep--the final humiliation. His mother had
suspected her son's sexual inclinations years before and pre-
tends to ignore what she has seen. Meanwhile, Lluis, lawyer
by day, joins an anarchist group seeking to overthrow the
regime of Primo de Rivera. One evening, he and his "family",
set out to dynamite a train carrying the leaders to Barcelona.
The explosion fails, the insurgents are routed and Lluis is
jailed by the Civil Guard.

Eventually, the killer of the transvestite is revealed
as a local sailor. Lluis has already taken vengeance upon
Armengol; he steals drugs from a local pharmacy and frames
the drug dealer by hiding this cache in the billiard hall Armengol
owns. Armengol is arrested and charged, but denies the
theft; he accuses Lluis of "anarchist" activities. It is, nevertheless, only coincidental that the Civil Guard has Lluis under
surveillance and discovers his attempt to blow up the train
carrying Primo de Rivera. Shooting it out with the police,
Lluis and his lover are captured and condemned to death before the firing squad. Before Lluis-Flor de Otoño's execution,
his mother visits him. In an extremely emotional scene,
sensitively played, she hands her son a compact and lipstick.
Lluis makes himself ready for the firing squad, embraces
his lover and dies with his/her anarchist compatriots.

A Man Called Autumn Flower is, next to Torment,
Olea's best film thus far. He truly captures the spirit of
the gay Catalonian world circa 1930-31 and elicits a beautifully modulated performance from José Sacristán, one of
Spain's foremost character actors who usually specializes in
farcical roles. The film is very entertaining and fascinating
when the "show business" numbers of the transvestites is on
screen. Olea carefully researched the songs, the details for
the decor and the costuming in order to present this elegant
and decadent view of this hidden aspect of Catalonian society.
Homosexuality was always a taboo subject under the Franco
regime, but with the dictator's death, Olea was able to film
this extremely sensitive story he wrote with Rafael Azcona,
also known as one of the best screenwriters in Spain today.

Presently working on an original screenplay entitled Inquisición de brujas or Akelarre or Witch Hunt, set in Northern Spain during the seventeeth century, Olea has once again turned to a traditional recreation of the past. His best films are those which deal realistically and somewhat nostalgically with periods of Spanish history. When he tries to film stories about contemporary life, his films lack the grandeur, color and style of the true artist. His most interesting films are always shot in color and in the Basque country where he was born. He feels at home in Northern Spain and his new scenario about witchcraft set in the Basque region, one hopes, will confirm the marvelous talent and professionalism of this prolific director. 7

Bibliography

Besa, Peter. "Review of La casa sin fronteras." Variety (May 3, 1972), 20.

Besa, Peter. "Review of Tormento." Variety (Sept. 7, 1974), 18.

Besa, Peter. "Review of Tormento." Variety (Sept. 25, 1974), 16, 18.

Castro, Antonio. "Entrevista con P. Olea." Dirigido por (Mar. 1977), 16-21.

Declos, Tomás. "Review of Pim, pam, pum..." Dirigido por (Oct. 1975), 31-32.

Montejo, Rafael. "Una superproducción española: Pim, pam, pum..." Cinema 2002 (Sept. 1975), 52-54.

Navacerrada, Manolo. "Entrevista con P. Olea." Cine estudio (July 1973), 52-64.

"Gritos y murmullos: Pedro Olea." Cine estudio, No. 125 (Oct. 1973). Entire issue devoted to the films and career of Pedro Olea.

Strat. "Review of Akelarre." Variety (Mar. 7, 1984), 368.

Chapter 16

BASILIO MARTIN PATINO (1930)

Filmography

Short Films: 1959-60--Tarde de domingo; 1960--El noveno; 1961--Torerillos.

Feature Films: 1965--Nueve cartas a Berta; 1969--Del amor y otras soledades; 1971--Canciones para después de una guerra; 1974--Queridísimos verdugos (Dearest Executioners); 1975-76--Caudillo.

A native of the province of Salamanca, Basilio Martín Patino was born in Lumbrales, a dry and austere town, in 1930. His parents were both teachers and the young Patino spent his innocent years in Lumbrales during the throes of the Spanish Civil War. After the war, he enrolled in the University of Salamanca for a degree in Liberal Arts and graduated with a major in Philosophy. During his university years, he founded the Salamanca Film Club which, in 1956, organized the first Salamancan Film Congress. He also founded and wrote film criticism for Cinema universitario, the only university film magazine at that time in Salamanca. (Unfortunately, after eleven issues, it ceased publication in 1963.) Influenced by the rising careers of Juan Antonio Bardem and Luis García Berlanga, Patino proceeded to enroll in the National Film School. He moved to Madrid in 1955 and in 1960 received his degree in Film Direction when he completed his short subject, Tarde de domingo, for his practicum. He subsequently made two other documentary shorts which were financially successful, and filmed some commercials for Spanish television.

When asked to describe the kinds of films he makes, Patino characterized his work as "purely personal cinema."[1] "I do what interests me, and documentaries interest me most."[2]

Patino began his filming of features in 1965 when his Nueve cartas a Berta was released to a clamoring public that insured its commercial success. It starred Emilio Caba as Lorenzo and Mari Carillo as Lara, and Patino showed he was very much influenced by Jean-Luc Godard, making Spain's first really "modern" film in the mid-1960s. The film tells Lorenzo's story through a series of letters he reads in a voice-over, giving his bitter impressions of student life, his family, his aims in life in a provincial city. The film shows Lorenzo in conflict with two Spains: the placid, conformist one represented by his family and the politically and intellectually engagé one of his girl friend and comrades. Cartas has many of the overtones of a documentary and has been viewed as a pseudo-autobiographical statement by Patino. Patino has a special fondness for Nine Letters to Berta since it was his first feature film and an outstanding commercial success. It won First Prize at the San Sebastián Film Festival in 1965, although it was first shown in Madrid in 1967. Vicente Molina-Foix called Cartas a "rare political film in which ideas prevail over description."3

Del amor y otras soledades (Love and Other Solitudes, 1969), which starred Carlos Estrada and Lucia Bose (of Juan Bardem's famous Death of a Cyclist), again features an upper middle-class Spanish woman in the throes of a matrimonial crisis. The film had resonances of Bose's own marital problems; she had just separated from her husband, Luis Dominguín. Bose's performance as a woman undergoing personal frustrations appeared even more profound in light of her own personal crisis. The film tried vainly to deal with the deeper problems of a marriage going out of control. Patino realized that feature films based upon fictional scenarios were not the best vehicles for him to reveal truths about Spain. He could no longer tolerate the crass commercialism of the Spanish film industry and turned his attentions to filming only documentaries.

Canciones después de una guerra (Songs After a War, 1971) is an exploration into the enigmas of the Spanish Civil War in which Patino deals with all the pain and nostalgia of those fateful war years. Songs opens with Franco's entry into Madrid in 1939. The rest of the film is an "ironic juxtaposition of newsreel glimpses of the harsh years from 1939 to 1954 and highlights the popular songs of the time."4 The feature had been on the Spanish censors' list of "strictly for-

---

Opposite, two scenes from Patino's Nueve cartas a Berta (1965). Above, Mari Carillo and Emilio G. Caba.

Carlos Estrada and Lucia Bose in <u>Del amor y otras soledades</u>
(1969).

bidden films" but finally achieved release in November of
1976 in Barcelona, and by Christmas time in Madrid.   Originally produced for $70,000 in 1971, it grossed 1.5 million
dollars by the end of 1976.   Patino's visual documentary style
consists of a lightning-fast montage of newspaper clippings,
newsreel footage, ads, collages, documentary material and
hand-colored frames.   The soundtrack contains music evocative of the era, Spanish songs that were popular hits of the
late 1930s and 1940s.

Despite the great commercial success of <u>Songs</u>, Patino
had to continue to work underground, since his documentaries
were always critical of the Franco regime.   "Either I could
play ball with the government or I could work freely, by my-
self.   I chose the latter way."[5]   Patino felt he had to rebel
and since finances were never a problem (he always had
wealthy friends to invest in his films), he began shooting
<u>Queridísimos verdugos</u> (<u>Dearest Executioners</u>) in 1972-73,
"his most realistic and controversial film."[6]

<u>Queridísimos verdugos</u>, aptly subtitled <u>Vil garrote</u>
(<u>Vile Garrote</u>), is another incisive documentary condemning
capital punishment by garroting in Spain.   The film is based
upon interviews with three official executioners still living in

the country, and explores their personal lives and their work.
Patino gives his audience a strong, unflinching, historical,
psychological and sociological view of garroting and the need
for law reform. Once again, he combines a variety of media
effects. To shoot the film in color, Patino secretly brought
in a small camera crew from Portugal and photographed the
interviews and the locales of the executions. One of the executioners died by the time Patino completed his documentary
but it was not too difficult to find someone to take his place.
The film recounts the testimony of criminals and parents of
criminals, petitions for clemency that are ignored, legal has-
sles, and also gives an historical perspective on the origins
of garroting. It is a long and serious two-hour documentary
(it was cut from its original four-hour length, which gives
the present version an erratic quality and disjointed montage,
causing lapses in continuity) that demonstrates a type of very
personal, intense cinema, which is Patino's stock-in-trade.

Married, with one teenage son and living in Madrid,
Patino himself is a very intense person.[7] "I am even more
neurotic than Victor Erice,"[8] he told me somewhat comically.
"But I do not want to popularize Spanish cinema as a whole,
like José Luis Borau, one of my professors. I want to make
extremely personal films."[9] Like Erice, Patino told me of
his distaste for interviews, even though he appears in José
María Gironella's Cinco hombres ante Franco (Five Men Before Franco). After many detrimental experiences with the
Spanish government, he has little regard for the press. When
he made Caudillo in 1975, he had intended to do a two-part
film. Franco's life until 1939 was completed, but he has
since lost interest in doing the second part.[10] Patino feels
Caudillo is the best film he ever made. Characterized as
a "savage revisionist attack,"[11] and assembled with the same
matrix of media material, including voice-over memories by
Pablo Neruda and George Orwell among others, Caudillo was
filmed in the same manner as Songs and Executioners. It
is the ultimate testament of the Civil War--a film about how
heroes die and dictators are made. The film has been picked
up by an American film distributor and the 111-minute version
has been used for educational instruction throughout the U.S.
Ironically, it has received greater distribution here than in
the country of its origin.

Patino's forte as a documentary filmmaker lies in his
ability to show the crude realities of Spanish Fascism (Songs),
the penal code (Executioners), and dictatorship (Caudillo). He
is a very shy, reclusive person whose chief film interests are
his collection of old projectors and magic lanterns and the big

Portrait of General Francisco Franco as seen in Patino's documentary, Caudillo (1976).

Hollywood musicals of the 1930s and 1940s with their escapist qualities. Although Caudillo was his last film and received a somewhat mixed reception by the Spaniards who saw it, Patino intends now to study video techniques in New York City before embarking upon another screenplay. [12] He considers himself an extremely personal auteur and not a commercial hack. One hopes his future documentary projects will be met more receptively by the Juan Carlos government and that Patino will be encouraged to exercise his talents fully as a truthful purveyor of Spanish history and contemporary society.

Bibliography

Bilbatur, M., "Conversación con B. M. Patino." Nuestro cine No. 52, (1966), 8-21.

Besa, Peter. "Rebirth of Helmer Patino, Condemned Under Franco." Variety (Jan. 12, 1977), 64.

Company, Juan M. "Habla Patino." Dirigido por (Nov. 1976), 27-29.

Castro, A. "Reseña de Queridísimos verdugos." Dirigido por (May 1977), 30.

Castro, A. "Review of Caudillo." Dirigido por No. 49, 61-62.

Escudero, Isabel. "Review of Canciones para después de una guerra." Cinema 2002 (Jan. 1977), 22-23.

Heredero, Carlos. "Review of Queridísimos verdugos." Cinema 2002 (June, 1977), 26-27.

Markham, James M. "Movies in Spain Starting to Deal with Civil War." New York Times (Nov. 28, 1976), 15.

Siles, José M., "Patino y sus verdugos." Cinema 2002 (June 1977), 56-58.

Pamphlet

Pérez Millián, Juan Antonio & Francin Sánchez, Ignacio. "Revisión de la obra de Basilio Martín Patino." (Salamanca: University of Salamanca, July 1980), 14p.

Chapter 17

MIGUEL PICAZO (1927)

Filmography

Short Films: 1960--La mañana de domingo; Las motos; Habitación de alquiler.

Feature Films: 1964--La tía Tula (Aunt Tula); 1967--Oscuros sueños de agosto (Dark Dreams of August); 1976--El hombre que supo amar; Homenaje a Andrea; 1977--Los claros motivos del deseo (Clear Motives of Desire).

Miguel Picazo's great reputation in Spanish cinema is based upon his filming of Miguel de Unamuno's outstanding novella, La tía Tula, in 1964. Since then, his career as a director can be characterized as erratic. Born in Cazorla in the province of Jaen (southern Spain) on March 27, 1927, Picazo is very proud of his Andalusian heritage. A bachelor, diabetic and obsessively overweight, he had lost some sixty kilos recently, although he still gives the impression he is playing the role of a Spanish Orson Welles.[1] Like so many of his colleagues, Picazo took a degree in Law at the University of Guadalajara and wrote film criticism for the local radio station. He also helped organize the Cine-Club Estudio there as well as one at the University of Madrid in the late 1950s. Receiving his degree from the National Film School in 1960 and presenting Habitación de alquiler for his practicum, he was appointed Adjunct Professor of Film Direction.

Habitación de alquiler (Room for Rent) is a fascinating short feature dealing with a young man who arrives in Madrid, looking for his girl friend who is studying ballet. Because he does not have her address, he moves into a furnished room in the neighborhood where he believes she is living. Alone and lost in the big city, the young man commits suicide, turning on the gas in his room, while the landlady of the boarding house is telling a friend that the girl he was looking for had committed suicide some weeks earlier. Picazo's tale of love, frustration and suicides serves as an index to his enormous interest into the psychological motivations of his characters, which is the singular and outstanding quality in all his films.

For many years, Picazo's name was largely forgotten and his activity was virtually reduced to infrequent and undistinguished television jobs.[2] Suddenly, in 1963-64, he directed La tía Tula, starring Aurora Batista, and his reputation soared. Tía Tula is always cited as one of the best ten or fifteen Spanish films ever made. It was Picazo's first

Carlos Estrada and Aurora Batista in Picazo's La tía Tula (Aunt Tula, 1964).

full-length film and it deservedly won the first prize at the San Sebastián Film Festival in 1964. Tula is a splendid recreation of provincial Spanish life at the turn of the century and an implacable and rigorous psychological analysis of an old maid dominated by sexual, religious and ideological frustrations. It is "an interesting combination of contemporary and old-fashioned plotting with Freudian undertones and mid-Victorian overtones to heighten the domestic drama."[3] Picazo elevates Tula's frigidity and personal tragedy to a representation of women not only in Spain but universally.

Freely adapted from Miguel de Unamuno's 1921 novella, Tula deals with a thirty-one year old unmarried woman whose sister had just passed away. She decides to bring her brother-in-law (a bank employee) and his two children into her home. As she takes over the management of their lives, she gradually usurps the privileges of her brother-in-law (remarkably well-played by Carlos Estrada) and his children. She acts as a wife-mother figure, but does not accept the sexual commitments and maternal responsibilities of her new role. Her brother-in-law, Ramiro, is attracted to Tula as she dotes on his children, but she spurns his affections. She is also critical of his interest in other women. As Ramiro's sexual frustration grows, he attempts to rape Tula. Tula's priest advises her to marry Ramiro. When she is ready to agree, we discover Ramiro is paying court to another woman (Tula's nubile cousin) and obtaining his sexual favors elsewhere. La tía Tula is an excellent film which demonstrates the sexual hypocrisy and middle-class bigotry in Spain in the early twentieth century. Tula will remain one of the eternal "aunts" Spanish society seems to mass-produce, women devoted to "virtue" and "duty" and afraid to live their own lives to the fullest. Tula has indeed been robbed of her love, her husband, children, everything. This inspired first feature film is touchingly played by all its actors, including the children. Picazo gives us such rich details that they transcend the plot and enrich it with marvelous moments of revelation. For example, the bantering of Ramiro's children with their aunt, or Tula's tender care for Ramiro when the latter is ill, are scenes expressed in such detail that they give credibility and naturalness to the fictional work. One critic felt that Aurora Batista was "too attractive, too vivacious to be completely believable."[4] Picazo considers himself a psychologist and claims he never has difficulty with actors, even foreign ones, because he is the director and he explains everything to them; then, they shoot the script after rehearsal. Batista's performance was one of the best he ever got from any actor.[5]

Since 1965, Picazo has dedicated himself to working in television, although in 1967 his film Oscuros sueños de agosto (Dark Dreams in August), made on a shoestring, was considered such a disaster by Spanish critics that it has hardly been shown in Spain or elsewhere.

El hombre que supo amar (The Man Who Knew How to Love), made in 1976, was also lambasted by the critics, the censors and the church, and it too quickly disappeared from Spanish screens. Although it starred Viveca Lindfors, Sonia Bruno and Julián Mateos, it was a very poor biography of St. John. Picazo's larger theme was to show man's

incapacity for giving and obtaining real love because of the
rigors imposed on people in society.

His last film thus far was originally titled Homenaje
a Andrea (Homage to Andrea) when it was released in Madrid
in 1976. But censorship problems prevented its producer,
José Frada, from keeping the film in circulation. After bow-
ing to the censors and making the necessary cuts, Homage
was released the following year with a new title: Los claros
motivos del deseo (Clear Motives of Desire).

Dealing once again with people's capacity or incapacity
for finding real love, this time in contemporary society,
Motivos was shot in color and Cinemascope. Acted by two
teenagers, Cristina Ramón as Andrea and Emilio Segrist as
Javi, the film relates the coming of age of a young woman
guitarist, her homosexual brother and their mutual boyfriend.
Motivos opens at the local neighborhood swimming pool where
Andrea is sexually molested underwater by Javi. To retali-
ate, Andrea starts rumors that he is a homosexual. Javi
takes vengeance on Andrea by agreeing to meet her brother,
a known homosexual who makes a pass at Javi. After luring
and leading him on, Javi beats Andrea's brother brutally, to
end the gossip about his own lack of masculinity.

Enroute to a guitar recital in Madrid, Andrea meets
Javi by chance on the local train and he brutally attacks her.
However, Andrea, somewhat repressed sexually, finds Javi
attractive and they begin to pet heavily. Because they are
minors, they cannot even enter an "illegal" hotel where they
would like to spend a few hours and make love. But as they
return home to Guadalajara on the Costa Brava Express, Javi
and Andrea make love standing up in the WC in a very long,
sensual scene. Upon their arrival, Javi tells Andrea that he
never wants to see her again, that he has deliberately seduced
and deceived her. Javi's girl friend is waiting for him with
open arms at the station as the train pulls in. Depressed
for several days, Andrea completely disrobes and threatens
to jump from the roof of Javi's apartment building. Dis-
traught through she is, she realizes nevertheless that suicide
is not the answer, and yells from the rooftop: "It was Javi's
fault. He's to blame!" As Javi comes upon the crowd around
his apartment house staring up at Andrea, he runs off in
cowardly retreat to some unknown part of the city.

Once again, Miguel Picazo has made an excellent film
replete with psychological perception. He shows the stupidity
and duplicity of teenagers and their lack of responsibility when

real emotions are aroused and life and death alternatives arise. Most critics felt that Claros motivos had an ironic title and that its penetrating analysis into teenage life was both enjoyable and realistically graphic. Motivos is indeed different stylistically from La tía Tula, but both films demonstrate Picazo's undeniable talent and uncompromising fidelity in portraying the frustrations of love in Spanish society.

Picazo presently works at the Ministry of Culture in Madrid and is doing educational TV films. He expects to direct his first stage play, Medusa y su buen chico by Luis Linza, sometime in 1982-83 and is presently writing a screenplay based upon José Pepe Vivanco's novel, Sombras suele vestir, which in turn is based upon a poem by the Baroque poet, Luis de Góngora. 6 At the Ministry of Culture he has been placed in charge of a program entitled "Campana Nacional de iniciación al cine para niños y jóvenes" (National Campaign for the Initiation of Film Study for Youth). Picazo had designed and co-authored a book entitled Cartilla de cine for this National Cinema Program. It is to be hoped that his educational efforts will not lead him too far away from his original métier as a perceptive director of frankly adult feature films.

Bibliography

Besa, Peter. "Miguel Picazo." Variety (Sept. 5, 1976), 50.

Crist, Judith. "Review of La tía Tula." Herald-Tribune (June 3, 1965), 42.

Crowther, Bosley. "Review of La tía Tula." New York Times (June 3, 1965), 18.

Robe. "Review of La tía Tula." Variety (Apr. 28, 1965), 7.

"A Virgin's Fury" (Review of La tía Tula). Time (June 11, 1965), 64.

"Entrevista con M. Picazo." Celuloide (Apr. 1968), 1-8.

"Review of Oscuros sueños de agosto." Film Ideal No. 208 (1969), 182, 188.

"Review of El hombre que supo amar." Dirigido por (Apr. 1977), 29.

Chapter 18

ANTONI RIBAS (1935)

Filmography

Short Films: 1965--Pintura española en el Museo Lázaro Galdiano; Danzas populares; El caballero de Olmedo; 1978-- Llibertat d'expresió; 1979--Cituat de Barcelona.

Feature Films: 1967--Los salvajes en Puente San Gil; 1968-- Palabras de amor; 1969--Medias y calcetines; 1973--La otra imagen; 1976--La ciutat cremada (La ciudad quemada) (Burnt City); 1978--Catalans universals; 1981--Victoria (Victory).

Of the twenty-one directors considered in this volume, Ribas is the only Catalonian other than Jaime Camino who has gained a glowing reputation for exceptional films within and outside of Spain. Although he has made a variety of films since the mid-1960s, his triumphs have become identified with the resurgence of the nationalist spirit in Catalonia.

Above, Antoni Ribas (photo copyright 1982 by Romi Montané, Barcelona--courtesy of the director).

His best film, La ciutat cremada (Burnt City, 1976), was the first one made and released in Spain to be spoken entirely in Catalan, and won the Special Grand Jury Prize at the Montreal Film Festival in 1976.

Like many other Spanish film directors, Ribas holds a degree in Law from the University of Barcelona with a major in Economics. Born there on October 27, 1935, Ribas began his interest in the arts as a playwright and scriptwriter as early as 1958, completing as many as five scripts for the Catalan cinema. Between 1959 and 1960, he wrote five more screenplays on a wide variety of themes and all were filmed successfully. From 1961 to 1964, Ribas worked as an assistant director on eight films before directing, in 1965, a fifty-two-episode color series for the Encyclopaedia Britannica on how to teach Spanish in the United States. Afterwards, he made three color short films, again for Britannica. These early ventures served as an apprenticeship for the feature films, he was destined to make.

His first feature, Los salvajes en Puente San Gil (The Savages on San Gil Bridge, 1967), about a group of actors wandering through provincial Spain, conveyed the sordid atmosphere of traveling companies and denounced Spanish social hypocrisy. The following year, he filmed a musical, Tren de madrugada (Early Morning Train), but he no longer claims responsibility for the film since the producer re-cut and mutilated his original work. In 1970, he made Medias y calcetines, also called Amor y medias (Love & Stockings), in which he humorously satirized the Catalan business man. Frustrated by his lack of success, he returned to the theater briefly and wrote and directed a play entitled Notas perdidas en el paraíso (Lost Notes in Paradise). But his attraction to film prevailed and in 1973 Ribas filmed La otra imagen (Another Image). Starring Francisco Rabal, it had a somewhat disjointed and stilted plot dealing with "a ménage à trois among blind people."[1] It was no better and no worse than the run-of-the-mill commercial productions being filmed outside of Catalonia.

When Ribas began to write and film La ciutat cremada (Burnt City), all his theatrical, screenwriting and early directorial experience melded beautifully together into a total harmony that resulted in his best and most commercially successful film to date. (The jury is still out on the box-office success of his most recent film, Victoria.)

Burnt City (1976) is a long, fascinating, three-hour

historical film in color depicting a group of Catalonian soldiers
returning from Cuba at the end of the Spanish-American War
(1898), their problems and their repatriation; it is also in-
timately tied to the Catalonian Separatist Revolt between 1899
and 1906. Using a popular device to show the parade of
Catalonian history marching by, Ribas concentrates upon one
bourgeois family as the film's microcosm. A soldier returns to his brother's family, bringing with him the fortunes
of war. This particular family runs a glass-blowing factory
and has two eligible daughters ready for marriage. A comrade soldier-in-arms returns with the brother from the war
and promptly falls in love with the older, red-headed daughter.
(There are some wonderful pre-marital sexual scenes that
would never have been allowed to be shown in Spain before
Franco's death in 1975).

Angela Molina plays the other, "dark-haired" daughter,
spurned by the soldier who marries the eldest daughter; the
elder brother becomes a political activist, a unionist, and is
almost killed at the film's conclusion after fathering four or
five children. Molina finally seduces her red-haired sister's
husband during a brutal attack by the Madrillian army against
a poorly armed group of union leaders and Barcelona rabble.
The clergy seems to side with the military from Madrid.
Convents are broken into by the Catalonian unionists and
skeletons of babies and a variety of sexual misdeeds are revealed.

Meanwhile, this nuclear family of glass-blowers survives throughout the war and life continues for Angela Molina,
her sister and brother-in-law, the father-in-law who owns
the factory and all the red-haired grandchildren.

Although I saw a version of the film dubbed into
Spanish, the Catalan language was not too difficult to follow
since the film's plot is quite transparent. Ribas is particularly good at emphasizing the strong separatist feelings in
songs and deeds that show the Catalonian movement for independence from Madrid (Castilla) as an appealing spiritual
effort but a tragic failure. The actors, particularly Angela
Molina, look depressed throughout the entire film. The brother-
in-law, his wife and her parents carry the weight of the development of the plot line.

Burnt City is well mounted, beautifully costumed and
designed, and lovingly photographed with great attention paid
to period detail. The film successfully counterpoints the
changing fortunes of this bourgeois family and the class conflicts

Two stills from Antoni Ribas' La ciutat cremada (Burnt City, 1976), featuring Angela Molina (top).

against the era of the separatist movement. It enjoyed a
spectacular success in Catalonia, possibly as a result of its
banning for two years by the Franco regime. When the regime
was still in power, no film in Spain could be made in any
other language than Spanish (Castilian); Catalan thus was a
banned language. Also, the film is highly criticial of cen-
tralized rule from Madrid. Perhaps coincidentally with
Franco's death and the foundation of the Catalan Cinema Institute, Catalan cinema is now emerging in and around Barcelona as a new artistic phenomenon. Ribas continues to be
very active, participating in the Catalan Film Movement and
helping to regenerate the Catalan cinema.

Burnt City and its predecessor, Las largas vacaciones
del '36 (Long Vacations of '36), by Jaime Camino, although
the latter was released in Castilian Spanish, are fundamentally alike. Ribas, like Camino, paints the Catalan scene
with wide brush strokes on a gigantic Cinemascope canvas
and concentrates on fine production values to portray accurately the regional beauties of Catalonia. "Catalans obviously
relate to the film because it is part of their cultural and political heritage and because it is authentically Catalan."[2]
Burnt City may well trigger a whole new surge of Catalonian
historical films. As it chronicles the events leading up to
the Semana trágica (Tragic Week) in 1909 when barricades
were thrown up in Barcelona and Leftists tried to topple King
Alfonso XIII's regime, it demonstrates how separatism, anti-
clericalism, Communist and anarchist pressures were precursors of later political developments leading to the Spanish
Civil War (1936-39). Ribas is now preparing a sequel set
during the years 1917-1923 which would touch World War I
and the lively Barcelona music hall scene in the post-war
era.

Like his fellow Catalonian, José María Gironella, Ribas
is exploiting the province's history and nationalism to create
a possible "trilogy" of films. The second film in the trilogy,
Victoria, began shooting in 1981. Produced by his own company, Tabare, S. A. , Victoria will have a hard time selling
tickets. Subtitled "La gran aventura d'un poble" (The Great
Adventure of a People), Victoria will be a three-part film
running a total of nine hours, and tickets will cost about $25
for the entire series of three films. Part One is called "La
locura del '17" (The Madness of 1917"); part Two "El volcán
del Tibidabo" ("The Volcano of Tibidabo"); and part Three,
"La razón y el frenesí" ("Reason & Frenzy"). Written and
directed by Ribas, with Miguel Sanz co-writing the script,
and starring Helmut Berger, Xavier Elorriaga, Norma Duval,

Scene from Ribas' Victoria (Victory, 1982), with Helmut Berger (r.)

Craig Hill, Teresa Gimpera and Francisco Rabal with Pedro Lavirgen and Carmen Bustamente as singers, Victoria promises to be one of the more commercially orchestrated spectacular events of Spanish cinema in the early 1980s.

After completing Victoria, Ribas intends to film two other projects dealing with Catalonian history; one takes place in 1952, based upon the Eucharist Congress celebrated in Barcelona, and the other is "a Catalonian film of black humor," about a Catalan bullfighter who works in a local porno club by night.[3] Ribas' stature as a film maker has grown considerably. With Burnt City, which was shown in the United States under the sponsorship of the American Film Institute in 1980, and Victoria, he is constantly proselytizing for a Catalonian cinema of quality and with historical perspective. He is also taking advantage of the modern Spaniard's interest in the past, Spain's history and its nostalgia values. Ribas is profiting from his fellow Catalan's awareness of his regional identity and the new liberalized climate in Spanish politics and government. He hopes to continue in his present direction, concentrating on the creation of a Catalan National Cinema, making commercial films that establish an identity for the people of the province. His is a popular cinema combining historical fact and fiction. Dickensian in scope, his broad canvasses of Spanish history, and a multiplicity of fictional stories with many characters make his films joyful pageants, appealing to the eye, the ear and the mind.

Bibliography

Book

Ribas, Antoni & Sanz, Miguel. La ciutat cremada. (Barcelona: Ed. Laia, 1976), 202. In Catalan with film stills.

Articles

Besa, Peter. "Review of La ciudad quemada." Variety (Oct. 27, 1976), 28.

Besa, Peter. "Review of Victoria." Variety (Feb. 22, 1984), 19.

Mosk. "Review of Victoria." Variety (June 6, 1979), 22. The author sometimes identifies himself as Mosk(owitz), G.

Puig, Llorenç. "Review of La ciutat cremada." Dirigido por (Sept. 1976), 35-36.

Riambau, Esteve. "Review of La ciutat cremada." Cinema 2002 (Apr. 1978), 44-45.

Rom, Marti. "Antoni Ribas y La ciutat cremada." Cinema 2002 (June 1976), 48-49.

"Entrevista con A. Ribas." Dirigido por (Dec. 1973), 1-5.

"Entrevista con A. Ribas." Cinema 2002 (Jan. 1979), 59-61.

"Ribas' Next Epic 'Victory' Uses 'Mini' Investors, Pre-Hype," Variety (Oct. 14, 1981), 72.

Chapter 19

CARLOS SAURA (1932)

Filmography

Short Films: 1957--La tarde del domingo; 1958--Cuenca.

Feature Films: 1962--Los golfos; 1964--Llanto por un bandido; 1966--La caza (The Hunt); 1967--Peppermint frappé; 1968--Stress es tres, tres; 1969--La Madriguera; 1970--El jardín de las delicias; 1973--Ana y los lobos; 1974--La prima Angélica (Cousin Angelica); 1976--Cría cuervos; 1977--Elisa, vida mía; 1978--Los ojos vendados; 1979--Mama cumple cien años (Mama Turns 100); 1980--Deprisa, deprisa; 1981--Bodas de sangre (Blood Wedding); 1982--Dulces horas; Antonieta; 1983--Carmen; 1984--Los Zancos (The Stilts).

      Other than Luis Buñuel, Carlos Saura is the only Spanish film director who enjoys an international reputation and immediate recognition as one of his country's most outstanding filmmakers. Like Buñuel, he is continually sought after for interviews, is still productive, and has had several books in Spanish devoted to his life and film career. Despite political and censorship problems, Saura has continued to make films in Spain and since Buñuel's recent death, he has become Spain's most prestigious director. Unlike Buñuel (to whose work many tomes have been devoted, in both English and Spanish), Saura deserves a chapter here because he has made some twenty feature films, most of which have been seen at one time or another in the United States and elsewhere. He is the only director in this book who has this distinction. Like Buñuel, he is heir to the tradition of esperpento, a blend of the grotesque and the macabre, and traumatic childhood memories of the Spanish Civil War pervade his films. An examination of at least one key film from each of three decades will sum up his contributions to Spanish cinema and demonstrate the path of his career--past, present and future.

Carlos Saura (photo courtesy Filmoteca Nacional, Madrid).

Carlos Saura was born in Huesca (Aragón) on January 4, 1932, the second of four children, to gifted, professional parents. His father was an attorney, his mother, a pianist. In 1935, the family moved to Madrid, just before the outbreak of the Spanish Civil War. Saura's films have been affected by his memories of this traumatic period of his life. Caught in the conflagration, he was taught to read and write by a priest related to the Sauras who took refuge with them during the war. He attended a high school run by Augustinian Friars in Gatafe, south of Madrid, but finished his bachillerato at a secular school in the capital. During his adolescence, he played hooky and went to see the great romantic films of the 1940s starring Loretta Young and Lana Turner, or the great adventure films like The Prisoner of Zenda starring Madeleine Carroll and Ronald Colman.

After graduating from high school, where Saura showed an aptitude for mathematics, he enrolled in a program to be an industrial engineer, but realized early the error of that career choice. He was interested in photography from the early 1950s, when he earned a "bohemian" livelihood as a roving photographer at music festivals in Santander, Granada and elsewhere. He held his first one-man show in 1951 at the Royal Photography Society and two years later had another show entitled "Tendencies." At age nineteen, he was considered a thorough professional, good enough to prepare an entire volume on the regions of Spain, for which he took and collected thousands of photographs; unfortunately it was never printed.

Carlos' brother Antonio, a well-known abstract-expressionist painter, advised the floundering photographer to enter the IIEC (Instituto de Investigaciones y Experiencias Cinematográficas) in Madrid in 1952. The Italian neo-realist films by deSica, Rossellini and Zavattini were being shown in Spain at this time and had a profound effect upon Saura and many students who wanted to become filmmakers. In fact, Saura's entrance into Spanish cinema is significant because he was part of the development of the New Spanish Cinema Movement which had its roots in the Italian neo-realist style, the characteristics of which are evident in Saura's early films. Saura and his generation of filmmakers were judged to be the link between the films of Bardem and those of Berlanga. Roger Mortimore, the English Madrid-based critic for Sight & Sound, told me that "Saura is the only Spanish director since 1939, with the exception of Berlanga, who has remained true to himself."[1] At the same time that Saura entered the National Film School in 1952, he also joined the school of

Journalism at the University of Madrid, but he quickly dropped out of the latter, concentrating all his energies on film studies. He received his degree in 1957 when he submitted three short films for his practicum: El tíovivo (The Merry-go-round), Pax (Peace) and Tarde de domingo (Sunday Afternoon). The last film was a 35 mm. short in black and white, made with a hand-held camera on location in a dance hall often frequented by off-duty maids. Although Saura now considers it a "senti-mental rehearsal in the neo-realist vein, "[2] it contained ideas and techniques he would utilize in his future feature films.

From 1957 to 1964, Saura became a professor at the IIEC and later at the National Film School. During this period, he made another short, Cuenca, a 45-minute documentary in color that won several awards. In retrospect, Saura now feels that this documentary suffered because of its long and superfluous commentary. Saura is intensely interested in images, not narrative. Nevertheless, Cuenca may be con-sidered an experimental short made in the same way as an-other of his uncompleted documentaries, Carta de Sanabre, using hand-held cameras in the manner of cinéma-verité. (Just a few years before, Jean-Luc Godard's A bout de souffle [Breathless] revolutionized French cinema techniques with his use of quick cuts, jump cuts, freeze-frames and mobile hand-held cameras.) These short films and his experience in photography and teaching helped Saura to achieve his goal, the production of feature films, as early as 1961.

He began filming Los golfos (The Hooligans) in 1959-60. It reminded many critics of Luis Buñuel's Los olvidados (The Young and the Damned) and Godard's A bout de souffle (Breathless). It was a social exposé of teenage life and gangs in Spain of the late 1950s. Saura used his own brand of realism to tell the story of youths trapped by social circum-stances who would never succeed in life, a continual leitmotiv in Saura's subsequent films. Like the espontáneos of old, these teenagers from Madrid's slums try to crash into the world of bullfighting but become frustrated by their inexpertise. The cast was mainly non-professional, as in so many of the Italian neo-realist films. Los golfos was an important film for Saura because it broke with the tradition of escapist cinema, the kind of entertainments encouraged by the Franco regime. Saura helped to begin the movement toward creation of the true "art" film in Spain. Although Los golfos was largely unsuccessful, nationally and internationally, it had the dis-tinction of being the first Spanish film ever made entirely on location. When it was presented at the Cannes Film Festival in 1961, Saura met Buñuel, whose own production, Viridiana,

the hit of the festival, was banned in Spain because of its
anti-religious statements. Since Viridiana and Los golfos
were both produced by Pedro Portabella, the Spanish government frowned upon giving Saura another directing opportunity
till 1963. Looking at Los golfos today, however, "it stood
the test of time ... and still retains the force and freshness
which made it a landmark of the Spanish cinema of its day."[3]

Saura's next film, Llanto por un bandido (Lament for
a Bandit) was a color and Cinemascope western made in 1963
and starred Lino Ventura, Lea Massari, and Francisco Rabal
as El Tempranillo. Despite some excellent action sequences
that were precursors of the Italian spaghetti-western style
adopted by Sergio Leone et al., Llanto failed miserably at
the box office.

La caza (The Hunt), made in 1966, is Saura's most
important film of the Sixties and will be discussed in depth
as one of the three films which confirm the credibility, substance and stature of his career.

After The Hunt, Saura began a professional (and personal) association with actress Geraldine Chaplin and the
nature of his films changed from autobiographical to sexual.
Chaplin starred in his next three films: Peppermint frappé
(1967), Stress es tres, tres (1968) and La Madriguera (1969).
Absent from El jardín de las delicias (1970), Chaplin reappeared in five more Saura productions: Ana y los lobos
(1973), Cría cuervos (1975), Elisa, vida mía (1977), Los ojos
vendados (1978), and Mama cumple cien años (1979). Saura's
best film of the 1970s, however, is La prima Angélica (Cousin Angelica), filmed in 1974; it is discussed in depth below.
Saura's last film of the Seventies, Mama cumple cien años,
had its premiere in New York as part of the New Spanish
Cinema Festival held in January 1980 at the Beacon Theatre.

As Saura's career finds new strength in the 1980s, the
best of his films, Bodas de sangre (Blood Wedding, 1981),
involves us in passion and the dance. Deprisa, deprisa (1980)
and Dulces horas (1982) nostalgically recreate several themes
Saura had dealt with before and involve teenage gangs and
memories of his family life. Discarding these themes, Saura
returned to love and passion in Antonieta (1982) and the dance
metaphor for the operatic Carmen (1983), which was still
running in New York City well into 1984. Before discussing
in depth his three seminal films, La caza (1965), La prima
Angélica (1974) and Bodas de sangre (1981), his films with
Geraldine Chaplin and some others deserve our attention since
they indicate some of Saura's principal thematic concerns.

Top, José María Prado plays Luis in Saura's La caza (The Hunt, 1966). Below, Geraldine Chaplin in the director's Peppermint frappé (1967).

In 1967, Peppermint frappé was important to Saura's career since it established a working relationship with José Luis López Vásquez, one of Spain's most famous leading character actors; he appears in several Saura productions into the late 1970s. Peppermint had Chaplin playing the dual role of Ana and Elena. It was a story of sexual repression and eroticism, deceit and escape from relationships, and dealt with the meaning of love and the theme of woman as sexual "object." Molina-Foix sees Ingmar Bergman's influence in most of Saura's films with Chaplin. [4]

Stress es tres, tres (1968), dealing with a marital triangle, was made in cinéma-verité style. Saura exercised great directorial freedom in this film. Faced with a conflict situation, the three protagonists revert to childlike behavior, stripping themselves of the social conventions and communicating on a basic level. The characters in the film represented the opposing forces which existed in Spain of the 1960s: the surge toward a modern technological society in contrast with a compulsion to remain tied to the medieval ways of the past. Saura's film was unsuccessful in Spain and abroad, and he decided not to attempt again an "improvised" cinema using a hand-held camera in the manner of Jean-Luc Godard.

La Madriguera (1969), also known as The Den or The Honeycomb, starred Chaplin and Per Oscarsson as a married couple drawing closer together through a series of skits or charades until death becomes inevitable when one partner refuses to continue playing the "games." It is a fable of the mutual destruction of two very intelligent people. Chaplin plays the same character she played in Saura's two earlier films, but unlike Elena in Peppermint frappé she is bored with her husband, and unlike Teresa in Stress es tres, tres, she has no children to offset her boredom. The Teresa of La Madriguera is a lost woman, searching for a sense of self while being provided with a luxurious life style by a husband who loves her dearly. [5]

As Saura enters the Seventies, he turns to the esperpento, or the Spaniard's notion of "black" comedy. With El jardín de las delicias (The Garden of Delights, 1970), starring José Luis López Vásquez, Saura directs one of the most hermetic and unnerving symbolic works of his career. Garden is the story of a wealthy Spaniard who loses his memory in an automobile accident and cannot remember the number of the family's Swiss bank account, where the profits from its manufacturing enterprise are sequestered. To prompt his recall, his family recreates incidents in Antonio's life--his

joy with his mother, his first communion, his first love af-
fair--but all to no avail. Antonio lives on many levels of
blurred awareness and Saura's theme is that the key to memory resides in his childhood. Garden has an elliptical style
and contains so much ambiguity (undoubtedly because of the
danger of censorship) that its humor is lessened by the con-
fusions in the scenario. Nevertheless, it is a fascinating,
highly stylized, uniquely structured work, although its public
appeal in Spain or elsewhere was not great, despite a wonderful performance by José Luis López Vásquez and the advantages of color and Cinemascope. Garden's last image is
quite startling: when all attempts at prodding Antonio's memory fail, in the last scene all the family members are seen
on the lawn in wheelchairs. Perhaps Saura is saying that
all Spaniards consumed by greed or egoism are truly cripples.

Resuming his association with Geraldine Chaplin, Saura
made Ana y los lobos (Ana and the Wolves, 1972), which is
about a governess caring for three brothers in a decayed
mansion. For Saura the three brothers symbolized "the three
monsters of Spain: perversions of religiosity, repressed
sexuality and the authoritarian spirit."[6] Acknowledging his
debt to Luis Buñuel in connection with this film, Saura said,
"Buñuel was a little bridge between all of my cultural past
and the cinema that I was trying to make but did not know
how to do. Finding Buñuel was like finding an exit...."[7]
Of the three wolves, it is the religious one who devours the
young and free-spirited Ana. The contrast between Ana and
Buñuel's Viridiana, where the intending nun learns to live in
the world and participates in a ménage à trois at the film's
conclusion, is worth noting.

La prima Angélica (Cousin Angelica, 1973), the first
Saura film to receive an American theatrical opening in New
York, after winning the Cannes Film Festival Award of 1974,
is undoubtedly Saura's best film of the Seventies and will be
described in depth later.

Cría cuervos (Raise Ravens, 1975) brought back
Geraldine Chaplin in another example of Saura's fondness for
exploring his childhood memories. Cría deservedly received
the Cannes Film Festival Special Jury Prize in 1976 because
of young Ana Torrent's superlative performance and "Saura's
lyrical but perceptive examination of a child's world as seen
through the eyes of adults, contrasted with adults as seen
through the eyes of a child."[8]

Elisa, vida mía (Elisa, My Life, 1976) again featured

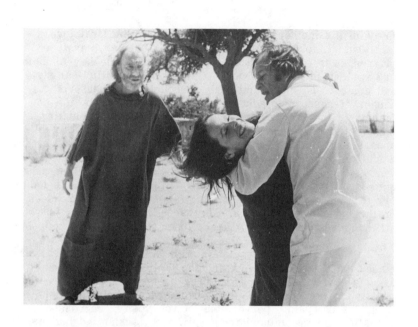

Top, Fernando Fernán Gómez and Geraldine Chaplin in Saura's
Ana y los lobos (Ana and the Wolves, 1973).   Below Encarna
Paso walks toward José López Vásquez in La prima Angélica
(Cousin Angelica, 1974).

Geraldine Chaplin, this time as the daughter of a famous novelist, played superlatively by Fernando Rey. After a twenty-year hiatus they reunite in an isolated house in Segovia to discuss their mutual problems. Elisa is running away from a seven-year marriage (her husband was unfaithful) and finds the foundation of her very existence threatened. Despite his success, her father, too, is unhappy about his life as the family reunites to celebrate his birthday. Elisa discovers that her father's latest novel is really about her own life and her relationship with him. Saura suggests a possible incestuous relationship but at the conclusion of the film, the father dies and Elisa is left alone with her fantasies. Saura regards Elisa as the most lyrical and most autobiographical film he has made, and the one closest to his own thinking. [9] Although Fernando Rey won the Best Actor award for his performance as Elisa's father, the film received very little international acclaim or exposure other than its appearance at Cannes in 1977.

Geraldine Chaplin talking to Ana Torrent in Cría cuervos (Raise Ravens, 1976).

Saura's penultimate film with Chaplin was probably filming at the time of their real-life separation. Los ojos vendados (Blindfolded, 1978) deals with the torture of political

prisoners in Latin America. It was his first film after
Franco's death. "Franco was like a wall, a barrier beyond
which it was impossible to advance. Now Franco is dead
and we can forget about him."[10] Although the film is strong
in its criticism of dictatorship and Saura takes many artistic,
political and professional risks, Blindfolded was not well received by anyone except Spain's intellectual elite. It is based
upon real events: two young men armed with machine guns
suddenly open fire in an audience which is listening attentively
to a masked witness giving testimony about torture in an un-
specified country, probably Argentina. The film is filled
with violence and terror. Saura uses explicit physical torture
as a metaphor for the hidden tortures of men and women
caught in different worlds but sharing common bonds. The
film is an angry protest against unpunished crimes and violence, overt and covert, which restrict daily freedoms.
Geraldine Chaplin plays Amelia, an actress, childless and
married to a dentist who occasionally beats her. Taking
acting classes, she falls in love with her instructor, played
by José Luis Gómez. In the play they are rehearsing, Amelia
is an informant undergoing torture to make her reveal the
whereabouts of her lover. Now reality impinges upon the
fiction she is playing. After packing her things and leaving

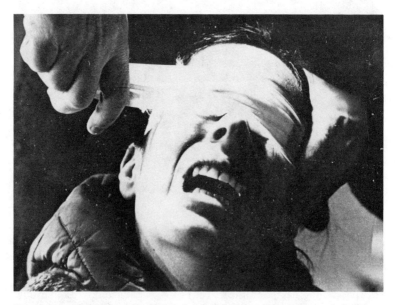

Geraldine Chaplin blindfolded in Saura's Los ojos vendados
(1978).

her apartment, Amelia finds that her lover's apartment has
been ransacked and he has been brutally beaten by an anony-
mous group that wants to prevent the opening of his anti-
Fascist play. As Chaplin, on stage, delivers her monologue,
she is murdered by machine-gun fire from the audience. The
conclusion's message is: how can one separate fiction from
reality or a stage play from real life. Saura says that art
and life are one and the same, and an actor must take the
responsibility of his words and actions, even if it means
death.

Mama cumple cien años (Mama Turns 100) is a complete change of pace from Saura's previous films. It is light
and comical, and perhaps because of this became a commercial success. It was one of the highlights of the New Spanish
Film Festival in New York City in 1980. Using the same
characters (and most of the same actors as well) from Ana
y los lobos, Mama examines this family a few years later.
(A comparison might be made here between these Saura films
and Berlanga's National trilogy.) Mama is Saura's last film
with Geraldine Chaplin and, like its predecessors, is a return
to the director's literary, poetic world about how the members of a Spanish family reunite for a celebration but intrude
into each other's lives. Mama contains one wonderful, almost
surrealistic, Buñuelesque dream sequence in which Mama
dies and a storm blows through the house, bringing her back
to life. An interesting film, Mama was nominated for the
in the Best Foreign Film category for 1979, but perhaps because of its serio-comic blend and a certain unevenness in
its direction, it did not win the coveted Oscar.

Deprisa, deprisa (Hurry, Hurry) did win the Golden
Bear at the Berlin Film Festival in 1980. It recaptures
some of the energy of Saura's first film about teenage life,
Los golfos (1962), and has been characterized as "a film
noir about juvenile delinquents."11 Deprisa is actually a
realistic and unstylized account of teenagers who snort drugs,
fornicate, rob banks and die unattractively--except for the
female lead who, very poetically, walks off into the distant
sunrise. Saura engages one's sympathies for the gang and
is highly critical of the Spanish police who prefer to kill
rather than question. The film makes excellent use of Madrid
locales and has a soundtrack of popular rock music. One
song especially, "I Get Along," unctuously pervades the entire film. Why this film won the Golden Bear remains a
mystery. Perhaps Saura began filming in this "new" direction
since it was made just at the time he split up with Geraldine
Chaplin, after they had lived together for more than twelve

Two scenes from Saura's <u>Deprisa, deprisa</u> (1980). At top,
José Antonio Valdelomar, José María Hervas Roldán, Jesus
Arias Aranzeque and Berta Socuellamos Zarco. Below,
Socuellamos and Valdelomar.

years and made eight films together. Saura moved from the
stylish penthouse he shared with Chaplin to a more "common"
part of Madrid, and it was there that he began writing the
screenplay of Deprisa.[12]

Deprisa represents a world that was completely foreign
to Saura. He rehearsed his unprofessional actors on video
for two months before shooting, and attempted to return to
the neo-realism of his early career while dispensing with
those "naturalistic" elements that had cramped his style in
the early Sixties. Deprisa does not set out to glorify gang-
sters, but to show how modern Spanish society can alienate
its youth and how, in this way, it becomes the real villain.
As art sometimes mirrors life, a real bank robbery occurred
just three weeks after filming and the details of the plan remarkably duplicated those of the staged atraco (heist) in the
film.

Bodas de sangre (Blood Wedding, 1981), which followed
closely upon the European success of Deprisa, deprisa, an-
nounces Saura's new direction for the Eighties. Dulces horas
(Sweet Hours), his next film, made in 1982, is a recherché
treatment of memory and hope with some Oedipal twists and
turns. The screenplay is somewhat obfuscated by a film-
within-a-film device, and that one can follow the continuity
at all is chiefly due to the sensitive performance of the actor
playing the leading character, who is seeking the answer to
his mother's suicide. Juan (played by Iñaki Aierra) hires
Berta (Assumpta Serna) to play the role of his mother in a
reenactment of his youth (which recalls Saura's ploy on Garden
of Delights). A series of letters written by his mother is
discovered in the possession of Juan's sister, and it is revealed that Juan's father had a mistress during the mid-
1930s and that his mother probably committed suicide over
her husband's infidelity. Juan, as a child, was the one who
brought to his mother the pills with which she poisoned herself, and he now feels tremendously guilty as an unknowing
accomplice in her suicide. Identifying his mother with Berta
(the actress plays both roles), he sends the young actress
away even though he loves her. However, as the film ends,
Juan is in the bathtub, his back being washed by Berta who
is now pregnant. Although they are supposedly married,
Berta has taken on her new role of wife-mother. Dulces
horas may be autobiographical and certainly it is a beautiful and
sensuous film to look at. The continuity of its screenplay,
however, sometimes eludes the most experienced viewer and
it makes no profound comment on Spain or marriage. Perhaps Saura wanted to have it both ways--to marry his mistress and his mother, as Pauline Kael suggested.[13]

Poster art featuring Antonio Gades in Saura's Blood Wedding (1981).

In examining Saura's directorial career from 1957 through 1982, it is clear that his three best films occurred in three separate decades: La caza (The Hunt, 1966), La prima Angélica (Cousin Angelica, 1974) and Bodas de sangre (Blood Wedding, 1981).

The Hunt is Saura's early allegorical masterpiece about three middle-aged men, veteran Falangists, reuniting in a provincial village in Castile, spending a hot summer's day drinking, reminiscing and hunting rabbits (and perhaps, each other). José (Ismael Merlo) instigates the hunt. He is in debt because of an impending divorce and living beyond his means with a younger woman, and his main object at the reunion is to secure a loan from Paco (Alfredo Mayo), a shrewd businessman. Paco brings with him Luis (Jóse María Prada), now employed at the former's factory. Paco is a weak, desolate individual, an alcoholic addicted to wine, women and science fiction rather than social conviviality or male camaraderie. A fourth member of the group, Enrique (Emilio Gutiérrez Caba), a teenage relative of Paco's, comes along for the thrill of the rabbit hunt.

Meeting at the local bar, the men proceed to a desolate farm house and hire Juan and his young daughter Nina, as well as several ferrets, to rout the rabbits from their holes. As the hunters prepare their guns, they reminisce about the Civil War and the excitement of hunting men instead of animals. After a few drinks, José asks Paco for a loan; it will cement their friendship, he says. Paco refuses but offers José a job instead. Saura is underlining here the conflict between José's aristocratic pose and Paco's post-war nouveau riche attitude. During the hunt, Paco kills a ferret; he claims he shot it accidentally but José feels he did it maliciously. As the hunt gains in intensity, the gunfire becomes more rapid. The smoldering hatreds and frustrations of the three men are triggered when Paco is hit by a blast from José's shotgun and he falls, mortally wounded, into a stream. Luis, enraged by the killing, tries to kill José by running him down with a Land Rover. José retaliates, shooting at Luis, but the latter, an expert sniper, fires a single shot at José and kills him instantly. Enrique, unhurt, is left alone in the midst of this carnage, trying to fathom the mystery of the inexplicable behavior of his three wartime comrades.

The Hunt is Saura's best film of the 1960s, a strong film with excellent performances. Not one inch of the film's footage is wasted on superfluous details. Each of the four

leading characters is fully developed in the powerful screenplay. The film's action builds steadily to an overwhelming
conclusion. We are repelled and yet held by the violence
we see on screen. Saura worked very well within the constraints of Franco's censorship policies, using his story of
four men out on a rabbit hunt as a metaphor for the Fascists
hunting down rebels during the Spanish Civil War. One of
the characters in the film finds a skeleton in a cave, which
recalls an incident from the director's own youth. The Hunt
is a powerful film with a grim theme and leading to a shocking conclusion. Saura tells his story simply, brutally, realistically. He is also critical of the lack of individual initiative
to develop Spain's natural resources and raise the Spanish
nation to the equal of other European powers. The Hunt is
often considered a cruel allegory because of its brilliant de-
tailing of killing, violence, sadism, and the ugliness of human
beings. It is, though, a flawless film, exhilarating, tense,
ruthless, brilliant, shocking, tough, fascinating, and superbly
written, edited and directed by Saura--his first indisputable
masterpiece.

Still working under the constraints of Francoist cen-
sorship, Saura directed another masterpiece in the 1970s,
La prima Angélica (Cousin Angelica, 1974), which won the
Special Jury Award at Cannes. Angélica is a triumph because
Saura finally brought together all of his youthful memories
into a surging, artful work which reveals as much about him-
self as his preoccupations with his memories of the Spanish
Civil War.

Cousin Angélica was shot in color in Madrid and Barcelona and stars José Luis López Vásquez in a dual role--as
the younger and the older Luis, participating in the recall of
his youth and also visiting his grown-up cousin Angelica.
Angélica is Saura's most literary film, very Proustian in its
textures and in its use of sight, sound, smell and touch to
recall memories of the past. In fact, "petites madeleines"
are dipped into Linden tea during the film as Luis, like
Marcel Proust in Swann's Way, delves into his past.

Initially, Luis comes from Barcelona to Madrid to
bury his mother's ashes in the family plot. (His mother
died during the Civil War.) Arriving at Angelica's home, he
discovers she is married and has a daughter, also named
Angelica. In fact, the same young actress plays both daughter
and the "young" Angelica in Luis' recall of the past. It seems
that Luis, presently a bachelor, is still in love with his cousin;
she, in turn, is having marital difficulties. Her husband is

a rather insensitive, gruff, materialistic Spaniard, in contrast
to the sensitive, understanding and spiritually effete Luis.
As Luis gazes upon the rooms, the furniture and his relatives,
he relives his past in Madrid, his adventures and love for
Angelica in the summer of 1936. Saura delights in the use
of flashbacks, Proustian triggers which recall his "lost" love,
how he and Angelica tried to run off together, to be stopped
by Falangist soldiers. There is a chilling scene showing a
bombardment of a religious school in which a little boy is
killed by flying shards of glass, which is probably based upon
a real incident in Saura's own lifetime. Saura's images of
the war and of his youth are "personal" ones and "dreamed"
ones. When he wrote the screenplay with Rafael Azcona, he
deliberately utilized Proustian references to create a literary,
artistic world of memories and images, a unique blend of
nostalgia and realism unlike anything in his previous films.
A retreat to Italian neorealism would have hampered this new
filmic style. In Prima Angélica, he cuts all the naturalistic
elements used in La caza, transcends their limitations and
evolves into an introspective, literary filmmaker of beautiful
and sensitive demeanor, perhaps inspired by the work of his
Swedish contemporary, Ingmar Bergman. And as in Bergman's films, Saura-Luis tries to recapture his past and revive
his feelings of love with Angelica in present-day Madrid. In
one beautiful scene, they meet in the attic, leafing through
old elementary school books, and discover poems written to
each other; but realize that their past is gone. Luis returns
to Barcelona enriched by his journey and explorations into
memories of the past, but decidedly a frustrated romantic.
Saura purposely avoids the steamy emotionalism of the Hollywood nostalgia films like the hugely commercially successful
Summer of '42 in favor of a cool but artistically sensitive
exploration of the Spanish character. Cousin Angelica is his
most controlled, unified, fluid and best conceived film work
of the Seventies, in which autobiography is merged with filmic
art. Saura continues this exploration right up into the Eighties with Elisa, vida mía, Mama cumple cien años and especially in Dulces horas (1982).

Carlos Saura emerges in the 1980s as a truly artistic
director, for the first time acting as interpretor of a classic
Spanish play, Federico García Lorca's Bodas de sangre (Blood
Wedding). While adhering to the drama, however, he chooses
to tell the entire story through the dance. Bodas begins back-
stage at a rehearsal hall. The actor-dancers are putting on
makeup and costumes, practicing steps. Saura as director
is a participant, asking questions, interviewing the dancers
in semi-documentary fashion, using his camera to capture
their pre-preformance conversations, thoughts, actions, jitters.

The star of the film is Antonio Gades, with his entire troupe of Flamenco dancers. In a long, rambling monologue, Gades, as he applies his makeup, reveals how he got his start in flamenco ballet. As the dancers prepare for the performance, we can see why Saura made a conscious choice to film Lorca's play as dance rather than as a literary or theatrical work. (He reprises this technique with Gades in his production of Carmen [1983], but with less impact.) Gades' choreography for Blood Wedding shows tremendous literary respect for Lorca and Saura felt that through dance, he could best reach the heart of Lorca's drama. This 67-minute film adeptly captures the drama--in the faces, the feet stamping in such throbbing closeups, the virtuosity of Gades and his troupe--of Lorca's tale of love, seduction and murder. The camera both records and participates in the telling of Lorca's tale of deceit.

One of the most thrilling uses of the camera occurs in the final climactic switch-blade fight, beautifully photographed in 360-degree camera turns. The camera "dances" itself. Sometimes Saura will begin a sequence with a close-up of one foot tapping and then cut away brilliantly, unexpectedly, breathlessly into a panning shot of the entire ensemble dancing a spirited fandango. It is a film of bewitching beauty, a spell-binding aesthetic experience. In nearly thirty years of filmmaking, Saura's career has matured extensively. Bodas de sangre blends his early naturalistic style with his later literary qualities into an imaginative and aesthetically beautiful film that transcends Saura's own sense of style, into something lyrical beyond himself. Blood Wedding transports us to a dimension of illusion, beyond personal significance into a poetic and spiritual union with Spain, flamenco, life and death. "Blood Wedding is an explosion of Spanish energy, a celebration of Spanish faces, bodies, voices, art, pride, sorrow."14

Saura's career is still blossoming. His film Antonieta, made in Mexico in color in 1982, stars Isabelle Adjani and Hannah Schygulla. This Mexican-French-Spanish co-production is about two women who meet abroad and recall memories of their mutual past love affairs and their relationship with each other. (It has yet to be shown in the United States.) Following the success of Bodas de sangre, Saura made Carmen in 1983, with Antonio Gades, Laura del Sol and Paco Lucia. Inspired by Merimée's novel and Bizet's opera and using Gades' flamenco ballet troupe once again, the film contains some spectacular dancing, performed without sets or props. If Saura had kept to his notion of a dance film made in the

Isabelle Adjani in Saura's <u>Antonieta</u> (1982)

high style of a Franco Zeffirelli-mounted opera set in the nineteenth century, <u>Carmen</u> might have been even more successful than <u>Bodas</u>. His error was to transfer the romantic plot the fictional intrigue acted out by Gades to a contemporary setting, Madrid society in 1983. When Gades murders his ballet dancer, Carmen, because of her infidelity (as Don José kills the Carmen of Merimée's novel), the scene echoes its nineteenth-century counterpart but has no reality in contemporary Madrillian society. Gades should just have walked away at the conclusion. Whatever faults his version of <u>Carmen</u> may have, though, Saura's powerful artistic growth over the past three decades is undeniable. His popularity, both inside and outside of Spain, continues to grow. He remains, despite his international reputation, content to work within the borders of the Iberian peninsula, where his films are eagerly awaited.

Bibliography

Books

Brasó, Enrique. <u>Carlos Saura</u>. (Madrid: Ed. Betancor, 1974), 346p.

Gubern, Román. <u>Carlos Saura</u>. (Huesca: Festival de Cine Iberoamericano, 1979).

Carlos Saura on location

Hidalgo, Manuel. <u>Carlos Saura</u>. (Madrid: Ed. JC, 1981).

Dissertation

Bartholomew, Gail. <u>The Films of Carlos Saura, 1959-80</u>. Northwestern University, 1982. Master's dissertation.

Unpublished articles

Higginbotham, Virgina. "Carlos Saura as Social Critic." University of Texas.

Kovács, Katherine S. "Loss & Recuperation in <u>The Garden of Delights</u>." University of California.

Articles

Besa, Peter. "Review of <u>Ana y los lobos</u>." <u>Variety</u> (May 28, 1973), 36.

Besa, Peter. "Review of <u>La prima Angélica</u>." <u>Variety</u> (May 8, 1974), 37.

Besa, Peter. "Review of Elisa, vida mía." Variety (May 11, 1977), 79.

Besa, Peter. "Review of Los ojos vendados." Variety (May 16, 1978), 22.

Besa, Peter. "Review of Bodas de sangre." Variety (May 29, 1981), 18.

Besa, Peter. "Review of Dulces horas." Variety (Mar. 3, 1982), 16.

Besa, Peter. "Review of Carmen." Variety (May 18, 1983), 16.

Besa, Peter. "Review of Los Zancos." Variety (Aug. 15, 1984), 15.

Canby, Vincent. "Review of Mama cumple cien años." New York Times (Jan. 11, 1980), C6.

Crowther, Bosley. "Review of The Hunt." New York Times (Apr. 25, 1967), 38.

Greenspun, Roger. "Review of Garden of Delights." New York Times (Feb. 12, 1971), 20.

Hawk. "Review of Stress es tres, tres." Variety (Sept. 6, 1968), 24.

Hawk. "Review of La Madriguera." Variety (July 16, 1969), 6.

Kinder, Marsha. "Carlos Saura: The Political Development of Individual Consciences." Film Quarterly (Sept. 1979), 14-25.

Lyon. "Review of Peppermint frappé." Variety (Sept. 6, 1967), 20.

Maslin, Janet. "Review of Blood Wedding." New York Times (Oct. 25, 1981), C8.

Mosk. "Review of Los golfos." Variety (May 25, 1960), 7.

Mosk. "Review of Deprisa, deprisa." Variety (Mar. 4, 1981), 24.

Schickel, Richard. "Review of Cría." Time (June 6, 1977), 76.

"Entretien avec Carlos Saura." Positif (June 1977), 2-8.

Chapter 20

FERNANDO TRUEBA (1955)

Filmography

Short Films: 1974--Oscar y Carlos; 1977--Urculo; 1978--
En légitima defensa; 1979--Homenaje à trois; El león enamor-
ado.

Feature Films: 1980--Opera prima (First Work); 1982--
Chicho, o mientras el cuerpo aguante (Chicho, or as Long
as the Body Can Stand It); 1983--Sal gorda (Bad Taste).

    Fernando Trueba has the distinction of being the young-
est director chosen to appear in this volume. Born in Madrid
on January 18, 1955, he studied Philosophy and Cinema at
the University of Madrid and was a student of José Luis
Borau. Fiercely independent, intelligent and shy, he is very
cosmopolitan and reads, speaks and writes several languages,
English and French among them. Despite his great interest
in philosophy, film studies took precedence and while he was
at film school he completed several shorts, including one
feature-length film in Super 8mm.

    In addition to making his own films Trueba has written
several screenplays with Fernando Colomo (see Chapter 7),
among them Könensonatten, an episode from Colomo's film
Cuentos éroticos (1979), and also collaborated on Colomo's
La mano negra (1980). Trueba also earns a living by writing
film criticism for the newspaper El país and the weekly Guía
del ocío. Because professional filmmaking is still an un-
certain career despite his recent successes, Trueba also
founded a new magazine for film criticism, Casablanca (homage
to Humphrey Bogart), now in its fifth year of publication.
Trueba is both chief editor and film critic.

    Opera prima (1980) was Trueba's first commercial

Fernando Trueba (l.) directing Luis González Regural in
<u>Opera prima</u> (1980)

feature and his first unexpected international success.[1] He
could not believe the positive reviews in Madrid or at the
Chicago Film Festival (November 7-26, 1980) but attributes
this reception to the love story portrayed in the film, "a
story that could really take place among young people anywhere in the world. "[2] <u>Opera prima</u> was quickly picked up
by Daniel Talbot for New Yorker Films and is generally
shown with a Saura film at one or another revival house in
New York City. Trueba feels that Saura does not represent
Spain or all Spanish filmmakers by virtue of his international
reputation. (The French call Saura <u>un monstre sacré</u>.)[3]
Trueba believes Spanish filmmakers need greater exposure
abroad and he will personally accept a contract to work abroad,
anytime, anywhere. He is not married, but shares an apartment with a woman who is very much interested in his career.
Trueba related to me his difficulties in filming <u>Opera</u> in
Spain, especially after 8 p.m. "Everyone takes a break at
that hour, everything shuts down. "[4] There is no concept of
overtime in Spain. No one cares about finishing the take.
In spite of these difficulties, Trueba managed to direct a 94-
minute feature in color and the Franco-Spanish co-production
became an international hit.

Opera prima has a simple story-line. Boy meets girl
one morning in Madrid at the Plaza de Opera subway station.
Matías, played by Oscar Ladoire, meets Violeta, his cousin,
played by Paula Molina (sister of the renowned Angela Molina).
They are two opposites who improbably attract and fall in love
with each other. Apparently Matías had lived with Violeta
and her family several years before, but now Violeta is nineteen, has her own apartment and is studying the violin.
Matías at twenty-five is a divorced journalist who lives alone
and would like to recapture with Violeta the happiness of
their youth. But so many things separate them. Violeta is
a vegetarian and Matías loves meat. Matías hates foreign
travel and Violeta adores it. (At one point in the story,
Violeta intends to make a trip to the ruins of Machu Picchu
in Peru.) Nevertheless they fall in love again and Violeta
seduces Matías. He moves into her apartment but Violeta
decides to leave for Peru in spite of her new-found happiness
with Matías. He is insanely and irrationally jealous of Violeta's
other male friends. When Violeta informs him of her impending trip, Matías insincerely tells her that it is a wonderful idea. But as Violeta leaves for the airport, Matías realizes he loves her too much to lose her. At the Aero-Peru
gate, Violeta decides to return to Matías. When she turns
around, they start running towards each other and embrace.

An extremely romantic comedy about intense, moody
young people who lead complicated lives and tend to complicate
them further with a variety of sexual liaisons, Opera prima
deserves its success because its actors are charming and
easy to look at and never seem to take the plot or themselves
too seriously. Oscar Ladoire won the Best Actor award at
the Venice Film Festival (1980) for his role. Shot in Cinemascope and color, the film captures the spirit of daily life in
Madrid from the "hippie" vantage point. Ladoire is perfect
as the skinny, foul-mouthed, cynical madrileño looking for
love and finding it with the somewhat corpulent and sexy
Paula Molina, who made her acting debut in this film. Opera
prima is full of youth, charm, scintillating language, delight-
ful dialogue. It is one of the best written and directed films
of 1980 and shows off Madrid and its young lovers to their
mutual advantages.

Matías may seem like a familiar film character to
those who remember Antoine Doinel in the François Truffaut
films, Love on the Run, Bed and Board and Small Change.
"Matías is the Madrillian version of all the Seventies' gentle,
angry young men in Western European films."[5] But Matías
has wit, a sense of humor and a beguiling self-confidence that

Paula Molina and Oscar Ladoire in Trueba's Opera prima (First Work, 1980).

his French counterpart seems to lack. Trueba also inserts
Matías as an interviewer into a world of the pseudo-literati
and porno film makers, all to fine comic effect. He seems
to share with Woody Allen an affinity for bubble-headed bum-
blers. This is especially evident during Matías' outrageous
interview with an American author, Warren Belch, who has
just published his first novel, A Trip to the End of My Anus.
(Sometimes, Trueba's humor and lampoons are a bit too broad
and off color.) Yet Opera can be so hysterically funny that
one sometimes cannot understand how this very amateur and
yet sophisticated film was ever produced in Spain. Gone are
the morbid metaphors of Carlos Saura and his recapturing of
the past and the Civil War. Opera prima is the first light-
hearted film to come from Spain and demonstrates a kind of
renaissance in Spanish filmmaking. It is the first Spanish
comedy à la Truffaut or Allen and its charm and wit perhaps
reflect the new post-Franco cultural and sexual freedom.
Women like Violeta are portrayed as emancipated, sophisticated, sexual. No tía Tula here. Sexuality and its variations
and combinations are all portrayed openly, easily on the screen,
and for the first time, in amazingly good taste. "Opera prima
is a light, upbeat comedy aimed at an articulate youth market."[6]

It is a marvelously controlled film, largely made up
of two-shots. It is also a wonderful example of classical
film-making, a tribute to Trueba's intelligence in not treating
flamboyantly such flamboyant material. "Spanish filmmakers
need greater discipline, a tightening of methods, a tightening
of spirit."[7]

Trueba avoided the temptations to "jazz up" his screenplay with excessive zaniness on the part of his actors or a
soundtrack that contained too many "hip" or "mod" or "rock"
songs and sounds. He succeeds in convincing us of the romance between Matías and Violeta, the cranky intellectual
and the earthy sensualist, because he employs directorial re-
straint. Although the origin of the film was a pun on the
words opera (work) and prima (first), Trueba decided to have
a musical prima (cousin), who lives near the "opera" métro
station, meet her cousin and begin their romance.

Currently, Trueba is co-authoring a new script with
Oscar Ladoire entitled Kodacrome, his supposed project for
1981. In 1982, he intends to film in Paris El sueño del mono
loco (The Dream of the Crazy Monkey), by a British novelist,
Christopher Frank, who writes in French. He is also working on a new screen version of George Axelrod's The Seven-
Year Itch, called tentatively, La Marsellesa, and hopes to

obtain the rights from Axelrod in the near future. Trueba is a young director to watch for in the future. He has brought humor into the sometimes airless world of the Spanish cinema. It is wonderful to hear laughter ring out at the movie palaces along Madrid's Gran Vía (Broadway) again. 8

Bibliography

Book

Ladoire, O. and Trueba, F. Opera Prima. (Madrid: Ed. Privado, 1981), 158p.

Articles

Antolín, M. "Review of Opera prima." Cinema 2002 (Feb. 1980), 46-49.

Besa, Peter. "Review of Opera prima." Variety (Dec. 16, 1981), 16.

Besa, Peter. "Review of Mientras el cuerpo aguante (While the Body Resists)." Variety (Oct. 6, 1982), 18.

Canby, Vincent. "Review of Opera prima: Portrait of a Madrileño." New York Times (Jan. 6, 1982), C17.

Castro, Antonio. "Entrevista con F. Trueba." Dirigido por (Jun-July 1980), 18-22.

"Review of Opera prima." Cinema 2002 (June 1980), 19.

Kehr, Dave. "The Last Week of the Chicago Film Festival." Chicago Reader (Nov. 21, 1980), I, 12-13.

Rickey, Carrie. "Review of Opera prima." Village Voice (Jan. 6-12, 1982), 44.

Chapter 21

IVAN ZULUETA (1943)

Filmography

Short Films: 1970-1980--Leo es pardo; Masaje; Souvenir;
A Mal Gam A; Babin; Acuarium; Primera parte; En la ciudad.

Feature Films: 1970--Un, dos, tres ... al escondite inglés
(1, 2, 3, ... Hide & Seek); 1980--Arrebato (Rapture).

Born in San Sebastián in 1943, Iván Zulueta studied
design and set decoration in the Centro Español de Nuevas
Profesiones for a brief period. He received a degree in
film direction at the National Film School, but began his
career in Spanish television and directed a weekly talk show
called Ultimo grito (Last Cry) for nearly two years. As part
of his apprenticeship, he moved in 1964 to New York, where
he studied painting and commerical art at the Art Students
League. After returning to Madrid and graduating from film
school, Zulueta began a varied career which included directing musical programs for television, designing record covers,
film posters, movie theatre facades, working as an actor and
directing many short films in Super-8mm. Sponsored by José
Luis Borau, Zulueta directed his first feature film for El
Imán Productions. Un, dos, tres ... al escondite inglés
(1970) is a comical musical and was his only feature film
until 1980. In the late 1970s he was honored with a special
exhibition of his posters for films, music festivals and rock
groups.

His first film, 1, 2, 3, ... , directed in the style of
Richard Lester's Oh, What a Lovely War!, was a zany,
tongue-in-cheek color film set in a "pop" art milieu. In it,
Zulueta suggests much, like Milos Forman's Hair, about the
"hippie" world of the Sixties, but 1, 2, 3, ... had no unified story; it was just a series of musical numbers strung

Iván Zulueta (r.) lining up his camera (photo courtesy Filmoteca Nacional, Madrid).

together, depicting the patina of life of Madrid's youth of
that era. It was a disaster. It could not be taken seriously;
its thematic content posed no problems and suggested no answers to the growth of the hippie movement or the psychedelic
generation. It was, however, beautifully designed and deco-
rated, perhaps Zulueta's only forté at this point in his career.

His preoccupation with modernity and the psychedelic
is evident in his short experimental films in super-8mm.--
Frankenstein, Masaje (Massage) and Leo es pardo (Leo Is
Brown), all made in the Seventies. Earning his living chiefly
as a designer, he worked for several ad agencies and did

Two scenes from Zulueta's Un, dos, tres ... al escondite inglés (1970). At top, Ramón Pons and Patty Shepard; below, Mercedes Juste.

publicity for many films, such as the Spanish revival of Luis
Buñuel's L'age d'or (The Golden Age) and Los restos del
naufragio (Remains of a Shipwreck), for which he designed
all the posters and lobby cards. Zulueta feels much affinity
with directors like Josef Von Sternberg, who literally designed
all phases of such of his own films as The Blue Angel and
Shanghai Express.[1] Zulueta prefers "experimental" cinema
to Hollywood's super-technological productions. In 1979, he
put aside all of his other activities to concentrate full time
on his feature-length dramatic directorial debut. The film is
called Arrebato (Rapture). It was shot in color and originally
ran over three hours. It was cut to its present 110-minute
format and was shown in November 1983 at the Spanish Film
Festival in New York City.

Arrebato reportedly captivated the youthful Spanish
film critics because of its originality and perhaps also because
it was representative of the newest wave of freedom of expression in Spanish films after the death of Franco. The
theme of the film is how drugs affect the vanishing romance
of a film director whose career is floundering. Starring
Eusebio Poncela as José, Arrebato might possibly be autobiographical, since we witness a young filmmaker shooting
a commercial "vampire" horror film in which he has little
or no interest. After several days of shooting, José returns
to find a former girl friend, Ana (played by Cecilia Roth),
waiting for him in his bed. He is upset by her presence
and they both "escape" their reality by shooting up on heroin.
Ana tells José about a mysterious package which came for
him. It is a 16mm. reel of film, and they watch it together
in José's apartment.

Suddenly the scene shifts and the audience is watching
a film within a film--about an eccentric young drug addict
named Pedro who likes to film scenes of nature at his home
in the country, outside of Madrid's city limits. Pedro has
also provided a cassette soundtrack with his film. We enter
two worlds: José's apartment where he and Ana use drugs
and make love, and Pedro's home in the country.

Fascinated by the content of Pedro's first film effort,
José and Ana set out by car to track him down. They find
his home and meet him. Pedro quickly makes love to Ana.
All three then watch Pedro's film, trying to discover the
mystery within it. It seems that Pedro is the subject of his
own film. We wonder, in Pedro's last reel, whether or not
he commits suicide.

Another package arrives at José's apartment in Madrid. It contains a key which opens a room at the Hotel Meliá. Set up in this hotel room is a projector containing one last reel of film. José switches it on and we watch him losing his own identity and becoming Pedro. Just as Pedro reacted in his own film, José hides in his bed, dressed in his coat, and is being watched (filmed) by a camera which goes on clicking, clicking, clicking, incessantly, until the final fade-out.

José clearly is in search of himself. His life was at a dead end as Arrebato began. He cannot find rapture from sex or drugs. His real "thrill" is the mystery Pedro provides for him. Pedro's film and cassette provide José with a new path to take; when he reaches the end of it, he is completely absorbed by Pedro's film and personality ... and madness.

Rapture is a beautiful film to watch, well-acted and plotted, and lovingly photographed. There is much hallucinatory suggestion and many scenes involving nudity and steaming sexuality. Yet for all its frankness about sex and drugs and the odd couplings of its young Madrillians, it is completely empty of thought. Some critics called it "amateurish and

Cecilia Roth in a scene from Arrebato (Rapture, 1980).

masturbatory,"[2] and others found it excruciatingly boring.
Rapture was not a commercial success in Madrid. (It ran
only two weeks.) It belongs, however, to the experimental
vein of cinema and to the aficionados of cult films like those
who patronize the Midnight Movies in Greenwich Village art
houses in Manhattan. Arrebato is in the same league as
David Lynch's Eraserhead or Tobe Hooper's Texas Chainsaw
Massacre or George Romero's Night of the Living Dead.
Perhaps if it were dubbed into English and its "rapturous"
comments on sex and drugs made available to American cinema cult audiences, it might be more of a commercial success
here than in Spain. At least in America it may find an
audience. One can commend Zulueta for trying to expand the
cinematic outlook and consciousness of the Spaniards, but
Arrebato and Zulueta are ahead of their time in Madrid.
Zulueta is clearly testing the limits of the Spanish censors.
Films that thrill but have no substantial ideas behind them,
however, no matter how rapturous the photography, simply
bore or go misunderstood by their audiences.

Zulueta expects to complete his next film by 1984. It
is tentatively titled Luz y fer or LolaLela or Lalo Lelo or
Los Lelos, an erotic musical-vaudeville. He seems to prefer
to continue making these playful, "personal" cinema films
that fascinate him. He also has an idea to make a film, tentatively titled Chupanieves (Suck-white), based upon Walt
Disney's Blancanieves (Snow White), a musical with the
Mondragón Orchestra. There is clearly a pun in the Spanish
title, since Zulueta envisages a Rock group playing the seven
dwarfs and forming some sort of militant organization set
against the power of the Queen. Snow White Sucks is certainly
a title representative of Zulueta's "black" humor of the Eighties.

Zulueta represents for Spain what "underground" filmmakers like Taylor Mead, Jonas Mekas and Andy Warhol
among others represent for New Yorkers. Although he has
made only two films, they are both showcases for his undeniable talent as a filmmaker. Unlike those of his "pop"
or "underground" compatriots, Zulueta's films are not made
on a shoestring. There is great professionalism in his directorial ability to utilize actors and the camera, and it gives
his films the "look" of better than average Hollywood productions. Zulueta, however, will work only on films he wants
to do, which has limited him to too few projects. Because
some of his themes were formerly considered outrageous by
the Spanish censors, many of his short films were confiscated
and lost. Zulueta still lives and works in Madrid. A cosmopolitan, extremely personal filmmaker, he is still in search of
an audience.

Bibliography

Besa, Peter. "Review of Arrebato." Variety (Oct. 15,
1980), 220.

Bufill, Juan. "Entrevista con I. Zulueta." Dirigido por
(Aug. 1980), 38-41.

Fernández-Bourgón, J. I. "La muerte trabajando." Casablanca (Oct. 1981), 55.

"Review of 1, 2, 3, ... al escondite inglés." Film Ideal
(Apr. 1970), 25.

"Review of Arrebato." Cinema 2002 (May 1980), 46-48.

CONCLUSION

1. Ten New Film Directors: Short Profiles

Although this volume treats twenty-one Spanish film directors alphabetically and in depth, it does not pretend to be comprehensive. There are many, many more Spanish film directors who are worthy of brief mention here. Most of them have made at least one commercially successful feature film shown in Spain, but possibly nowhere else. Yet, news of their films and careers has traveled to America and they are included here to inform readers of this volume about some new Spanish filmmakers and their films, which they may be able to see and enjoy in the future. My choices are completely personal, and ten are included in this section who seem worthy of note.

LUIS ALCORIZA's films appear in Madrid from time to time. His latest, Tac-tac (1981), is a brutally graphic film about the rape of a young woman doctor and her vengeance upon her attacker (she castrates him). Alcoriza deals with the torrid themes of machismo and emasculation in an overly realistic, graphic, but successful manner. His films have been shown in Mexico and some other countries.

ROBERTO BODEGAS' only film to be shown in the United States was Los nuevos españoles (The New Spaniards, 1974), a light-hearted but fiercely anti-American satire starring José Sacristán as an insurance salesman whose life is overtaken completely by American efficiency methods in a quest for the "top" salesman award of the year. No Spaniard survives the ordeal for the sake of the "Brewster Company." Bodegas' latest film, Corazón de papel (Paper Heart), starring Antonio Ferrandis, opened to successful reviews.

FRANCESC BELLMUNT is a Catalan who shares Antoni Ribas' separatist politics and, like Ribas, has made about eight films, some of them in the Catalan language. The most successful is La quinta del porro (The Pot Generation, 1981),

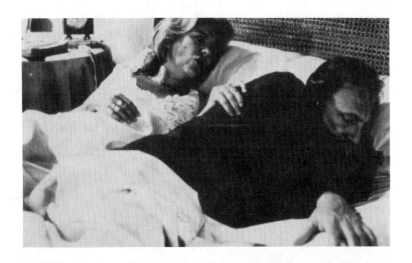

At top, scene from Luis Alcoriza's <u>Tac-tac</u> (1981). Below,
José Sacristán, Antonio Ferrandis, Amparo Soler Leal and
Manuel Zarzo in Roberto Bodegas' <u>Los nuevos españoles</u> (1974).

a comedy about Spanish Army recruits and their zany escapades in the service. Except for L'orgía (The Orgy, 1978),
Bellmunt's films have rarely been seen outside of Spain.

Another Catalan, JOSE JUAN BIGAS LUNA, is known
chiefly in Spain because of his film Bilbao, una historia del
amor (Bilbao, A Love Story, 1978), and his previous feature,
Tatuaje (Tattoo), 1976). Tattoo was considered a "pseudo-
porno" film by Spanish film critics and Bilbao was thought of
as essentially voyeuristic. Bigas Luna, who is obviously testing the new freedom in Spanish cinema, is a director whose
career bears watching in the future. His latest film project
is titled Reborn (1982) and was shot in Houston, Texas. Conceived as a religious thriller about born-again preachers, it
stars Dennis Hopper and Michael Moriarty, an intriguing duo.
It was shown in Spain in 1982, but has yet to be seen in
America. It is available, however, on videocassette.

ALBERTO BERMEJO is a young Spaniard whose film
style and screenplays are similar to those of Fernando Colomo
and Fernando Trueba. His first effort, Vecinos (Neighbors,
1981) is a very charming story of a young married couple
living in the suburbs of Madrid whose ménage is interrupted
by a next-door neighbor when the husband's jealousy is aroused
and cannot be suppressed. The husband takes another apartment in the same building and experiences extreme loneliness.
The film ends happily when husband and wife reunite after a
series of pseudo-romantic experiences. The film was shot
in three weeks. Bermejo's more profound comments on the
nature of "neighbor relationships" seem peripheral to the
shallow incidents of the screenplay. Where Trueba's Opera
prima benefited from a tightly constructed plot and superior
acting, Vecinos suffers because of the inevitability of its conclusion and the predictability of the characters' motives.
Nevertheless, Bermejo has talent and, like Trueba and Colomo,
is a director on the move.

RICARDO FRANCO is best known for his filming of
Camilo José Cela's classic novel La familia de Pascual Duarte,
simply called Pascual Duarte (1975). Franco reshaped the
tremendista or horrific sentiments of Cela's anti-hero into
an aesthetically artful experience, providing a catharsis for
the audience which is not present in the novel. Set in
a bleak section of rural Spain of the 1930s, the film
reveals the life story of a brutal but sensitive young man,
Pascual, who is a violent product of this destructive milieu
which leads him to matricide and death by garroting. Franco
has made only three films and was reportedly going to Hollywood

Garroting scene from Ricardo Franco's Pascual Duarte (1975), starring José Luis Gómez.

to direct, but to date he remains in Spain, working on other film projects.

EMILIO MARTINEZ LAZARO was co-writer of the script for Franco's Pascual Duarte and two years later directed his own first feature, Las palabras de Max (What Max Said, 1977) which was shown in the United States in 1980 under the sponsorship of the American Film Institute. Max, the protagonist, is a loner, trying to reach out to people for relationships. He is separated from his wife and must cope with rearing his thirteen-year-old daughter. The film goes on endlessly, dialogue after monologue after dialogue. We "hear" what Max says but never really get inside his character. Max, faced with the suicide of a friend, a liberated woman, or his teenage daughter, can hardly cope. He searches for tranquillity. His daughter finally deserts him for her mother, who is living somewhere in Madrid, and Max is left alone. Although he is intelligently played by Fernández de Castro, a sociologist in real life, the film sorely needs a professional actor. It lacks depth of feeling. All the verbiage

Two scenes from Mártinez-Lázaro's <u>Sus años durados</u> (1980).
Above, the "new" sexuality; below, student life in Madrid.
(Photos courtesy Stillman International)

is cerebral and comes from the "exterior" world of the characters, not from their hearts. Although there are some good scenes, the real center of What Max Said is emptiness. The film may appeal to an intellectual elite in Spain, and perhaps elsewhere, but the graininess of the photography and the poorly constructed screenplay detract from what appeal it might have. Max's words go in one ear and out the other. This director's latest film, Sus años dorados (Her Golden Years, 1980) is a rather pedestrian story of an older married man attracted to a younger woman and deals with the problems of sexual repression. Martínez-Lázaro is a promising director and it is to be hoped that he will not waste his talent on commercially popular themes.

JOSEFINA MOLINA and Pilar Miró are the only two well-known women film directors working in Spain in the industry. Molina has piloted two films, Vera, un cuento cruel (Vera, A Cruel Story, 1973) and the current favorite with Madrid's public, Función de noche (Evening Performance, 1980), a decidedly pro-feminist film about love, marriage, and loneliness made in a cinéma-verité style. It is reported to be a docu-drama similar in style to Ingmar Bergman's Scenes from a Marriage. Molina's film projects a new feminine sensibility never before seen on Spanish screens and proselytizes for the liberation of the European woman.

JOSE A. SALGOT, one of the youngest directors mentioned in this volume, is primarily known to Spaniards and Americans for one film he directed entitled Mater Amatísima (Beloved Mother, 1982), which caused quite a controversy in Barcelona and in New York at the Museum of Modern Art's New Directors/New Films Series that year. Mater was written by José Juan Bigas Luna and has a score by Vangelis. It deals with an unmarried woman (played touchingly by Victoria Abril) and her autistic child, Juan (played by Julito de la Cruz), who comes to dominate her life. When Juan's problem is diagnosed, Clara gives up her job as an engineer and devotes herself to caring for her illegitimate son. The two of them cling to each other for love and eventual salvation. Mater is a strong film with images of grief and loneliness that continually haunt the mind of the viewer. Salgot is currently preparing a film tentatively entitled Helénica.

MANUEL SUMMERS has been making films in Spain since the early 1960s and is known primarily in the United States for his Del rosa ... al amarillo (From Pink to Yellow, 1963), which was shown at the Museum of Modern Art's Spanish Film Festival in April of 1965. The "pink" section

Top, scene from Molina's Funcíon de noche (1980) with Lola Herrera and Daniel Dicenta (photo courtesy Stillman International); below, Julito de la Cruz and Victoria Abril in J. A. Salgot's Mater Amatísima (1982).

is a gentle story of young love among teenagers and the "yellow" deals with love amongst the elderly. His latest film, Angeles gordos (Fat Angels, 1980), made in New York, is about two young, unmarried young adults who are looking for love and, after a series of mishaps involving mistaken identities, finally find each other at the movie's predictable conclusion. Del rosa ... al amarillo was insubstantial as film fare and Angeles gordos is just as epicine, sentimental, vulgar and crassly commercial. Summers is commercially successful in Spain and Latin America, but his filmmaking is artless, tasteless, sentimental, coarse and trite. When the original Angeles gordos, dubbed into English, was shown on New York television, once could easily see why Summers' films appeal to a mass audience. Summers' "genius" is decidedly low-brow; his films are commercially viable but artistically stagnant. Every film industry indulges this kind of filmmaker because he corners the market on dumb and dull sentiment. Summers is not alone among Spanish directors in this respect. The movies of Mariano Ozores, Carlos Mira and Pedro Masó belong to the same kind of commercial cinema as Summers'. Summers' newest film, To er mundo e güeno (Everybody Is Good, 1982), using non-professional actors, opened successfully in Madrid and continues his pursuit of the sentimental motif on which his career has been built.

2. Short Takes: Five 'New' Directors

Apart from the preceding ten Spanish film directors whose films and careers have been briefly described, there are several more established directors whose films I have not seen but who have been working successfully for many years and whose names have appeared and reappeared in Peter Cowie's International Film Guide Series and Variety's Foreign Cinema Review columns over the past few years. They are Vincente Aranda, Cecilia & José Bartolomé, Fransesc Betriu, Mario Camus and Oscar Ladoire.

VICENTE ARANDA has been making films in Spain since the mid-Sixties and is best known for his science fiction films and his new "cinematic style," seen notably in Fata morgana (1966). However, La muchacha de las bragas de oro (The Girl with the Golden Panties, 1980), based upon the novel by Juan Marsé about familial dissatisfactions in Francoist Spain, and Asesinato en el comité central (Murder in the Central Committee, 1982), a political thriller about a possible

Scenes from two Aranda films: top, Victoria Abril in La
muchacha de las bragas de oro (The Girl with the Golden
Panties, 1980); below, Ramón Durán and Conrado San Martín
in Asesinato en el comité central (1982).

Communist takeover of Spain, are his best contributions to modern Spanish cinema. Girl with the Golden Panties reached New York in 1983 as part of the Festival of Spanish Films. Shot in color and Cinemascope, it starred Victoria Abril, probably the most popular actress of the 1980s in Spain other than Angela Molina. An aging writer who feels guilty because of his political past lives isolated while writing his memoirs in the late 1970s. One day, his niece Mariana pays him an unexpected visit. She is on drugs and has a lesbian lover. The relationship between uncle and niece begins slowly, but inevitably the girl insinuates herself into his life sexually. It is only afterwards that the uncle discovers the truth: Mariana is his daughter. The film is beautifully made and there are some extraordinary scenes of frank and open sexuality, but Girl with the Golden Panties is too long, and though high in style, has little substance.

CECILIA BARTOLOME with her husband, JOSE, directed another in the continuing stream of consciousness-raising documentaries about Spain after Franco. Entitled Después de... (After...), it was begun in 1979 and finished in 1981. Continuing the documentary tradition of Camino and Patino, the Bartolomés have made a controversial film that has hardly reached the Spanish public, since its commentaries are too close to the present political situation. This film marks Cecilia Bartolomé's debut after her graduation from the National Film School some ten years earlier; here is another woman tentatively entering the male-dominated Spanish film industry.

FRANCESC BETRIU is a Catalan who has made several features and excels at presenting a gallery of types, in the manner of Fellini, dealing with the lower strata of Spanish society. His most recently reviewed film, Los fieles sirvientes (The Faithful Servants, 1980), tells the story of a rebellion among servants somewhere in Catalonia when preparations are made for a huge party that never takes place (a somewhat Buñuelesque plot). It opened to excellent reviews in Madrid and Barcelona. His Plaça del Diamant (Diamond Square, 1982), based upon a novel by Merce Rodoreda, was disappointing and not very well received in Spain.

MARIO CAMUS began as a screenwriter with Carlos Saura and has been directing films since 1963. His best-known classics are Con el viento solano (Where the Hot Wind Blows, 1965), based upon the novel by Ignacio Aldecoa, and Los pájaros de Baden-Baden (The Birds of Baden-Baden, 1974). Camus is best known as a realist director in the

Scene from Mario Camus' La colmena (The Beehive, 1982).
Left to right, Francisco Rabal, Mario Pardo, Francisco
Algora, Luis Barbero and José Sacristán.

tradition of Giménez-Rico and Pedro Olea. His latest film,
La colmena (The Beehive), based upon Camilo José Cela's
1950 novel of the same name, was the biggest moneymaker
in Spain in 1982. The cast of the film, headed by José
Sacristán as Martín Marco, a poor poet who spends much of
his time at Doña Rosa's café, La Delicia, is enormous. The
film repeats the plot of M-G-M's Grand Hotel (1932) but the
setting is Madrid, 1943, post-Civil War Spain. José Luis
López Vásquez plays an ex-Communist scratching out an existence; Ana Belén is a prostitute working so that she and
her tubercular lover will survive the cold winter; Concha
Velasco reprises her "prostitute" role from Pim, pam, pum...
¡fuego!; and Encarna Paso and Fernando Fernán Gómez play
the parents of Victoria Abril, who is in love with the poet,
Martín Marco. Francisco Rabal, as another poet, comments
upon the lives of the more than sixty characters fleetingly
observed throughout the film.

One of the most memorable and funniest scenes in the
film takes place when the poets discover that the tables in

the cafe are marble slabs stolen from local cemeteries. Much
in the manner of Grand Hotel, Cela says "there is no solution to anything, a fact we have to accept even if we find it
disgusting. But it is not worth getting sad over it. Sadness
is an atavism, too."[1] As with the characters in Grand Hotel,
people come, people go, nothing ever happens. Spaniards,
like Americans, love to see film versions of their own classic
literature and Camus is one of the best practitioners of this
kind of artful transposition. His newest film, a commercial
pot-boiler, Guerrilla--Los desastres de la guerra (Guerrilla--
The Disaster of War), won the Golden Bear at the Berlin
Film Festival in 1983. Written by Rafael Azcona and Jorge
Semprun, it stars Bernard Fresson as a Spanish soldier,
facing Napoleon's armies practicing guerrilla warfare during
the Spanish Revolution, 1808. La colmena has already been
seen in New York at the 1983 Festival of Spanish Films but
Guerrilla awaits international release.

OSCAR LADOIRE, who began his career as an actor
and screenwriter in Madrid with Fernando Trueba's Opera
prima (1980), has become a director himself. His first film
was scripted and shot in the tradition of Opera prima and is
called A contratiempo (Syncopated Time, 1981). It is sometimes called On the Offbeat, and there may be autobiographical elements in the story about a married filmmaker trying
to recapture his youth, leaving his wife and embarking upon
an adventure with a fifteen-year-old girl he meets on the road
in Galicia. Following in the Spanish picaresque tradition, On
the Offbeat sounds very much like Bardem's El puente (The
Long Weekend). Ladoire's career still awaits further defini-
tion and evaluation.

3. Honorable Mention: Several New Wave Directors

PEDRO ALMODOVAR made an amateurish but spontaneous film debut in 1980-81 with Pepi, Luci & Bom, which
is about a group of teenagers who talk about sex, love and
drugs. It was a great hit at Madrid's Cine Alphaville and
the same theatre corporation (named after Jean-Luc Godard's
famous film) has now produced Almodóvar's second film,
Laberinto de pasiones (Labyrinth of Passions, 1982), which
emphasizes the perverse side of Pepi, treating sexual aber-
ration, transvestism and multiple sexual couplings on screen,
testing the new limits of Spanish censorship. Almodóvar is
following the Bigas Luna-Zulueta path of direct, experimental

Poster art for Oscar Ladoire's A contratiempo (Syncopated Time, 1983).

Cecilia Roth in Almodóvar's <u>Laberinto de pasiones</u> (1982)

cinema. His latest film, <u>Entre tinieblas</u> (<u>Amidst the Dark-ness</u>, 1983), recently opened in Madrid.

ANTONIO BETANCOR began working as an assistant director to Luis García Berlanga and Mario Camus after earning a degree from the National Film School. He received a scholarship to study film at the University of California in Los Angeles and worked in Spanish television upon his return to Spain. In 1978, he directed his first feature, <u>Sentados al borde de la mañana</u> (<u>Sitting at the Edge of Dawn</u>), then became seriously interested in Ramón Sender's famous novel, <u>Crónica del alba</u>, and began writing an adaptation of it for the screen. Released in 1982 as <u>1919: Crónica del alba</u> (<u>1919: Days of Dawn</u>), the film was an instantaneous hit in Spain, and de-servedly so. A continuation of <u>Valentina</u>, a film he shot simultaneously with <u>1919</u>, and which starred Anthony Quinn, Paloma Gómez and Jorge Sanz, it features the young pro-tagonist Pepe (of <u>Valentina</u>), now ten years later as played by Miguel Molina, an adolescent who forsakes his childhood love, Valentina, and encounters his first sexual experience in a cinema with Isabelita (played by Cristina Marsillach). Although the film was Spain's official entry in the 1983 Venice Film Festival, with an international star like Anthony Quinn as a drawing card it won no awards there and did not receive the wide commercial release it deserves, despite excellent

Two Betancor films: at top, Cristina Marsillach in 1919: Crónica del alba (1982); below, Anthony Quinn and Jorge Sanz in Valentina (1982).

acting and direction. 1919 was very well received by critics in New York, however, at the 1983 Festival of Spanish Films, although I prefer Valentina because Anthony Quinn captures all the nuances of his role as priest-teacher to the young Jorge Sanz as both move through the beautiful countryside of Aragón province circa 1939.

The documentary tradition continues strongly in Spain, as evidenced in JOSE MARIA GUTIERREZ' production of Arriba Hazaña (Long Live Hazaña, 1978), GONZALO HERRALDE's Raza, el espíritu de Franco (The Spirit of Franco, 1977), and the pseudo-documentary Soldados (Soldiers) made by ALFONSO UNGRIA. Gutiérrez' first film, inspired by a novel and co-directed by its author Mario Vargas Llosa, was Pantaleón y las visitadoras (Pantoja and the Special Service, 1976), a bristling satire of the Peruvian army, prostitution and politics. Herralde began making fictional films like La muerte del escorpión (Death of the Scorpion, 1975), before finding his true voice as a documentary filmmaker.[2] Ungria began his career as an abstract filmmaker, a surrealist whose films were cast in a Kafkaesque mode. Much misunderstood because of his pretentious style in films like El hombre oculto (The Hidden Man, 1970), Tirarse al monte (Dive into the Mountain, 1972), and Gulliver (1976)--the last two were heavily censored and never seen publicly in Spain--Ungria seems to have found his stride in the pseudo-documentary Soldados.

Scene from Jose María Gutiérrez' Arriba Hazaña (1978). (Photo courtesy Stillman International)

JUAN MINON and MIGUEL ANGEL TRUJILLO are a
directing team who made their debut with Kargus (1981),
shown recently in New York as part of the 1983 Festival of
Spanish Films. Both received their degrees in camerawork
at the National Film School and both worked on short films
before co-directing this first feature. Kargus is an episodic
film. A writer has just split up with his girlfriend. He

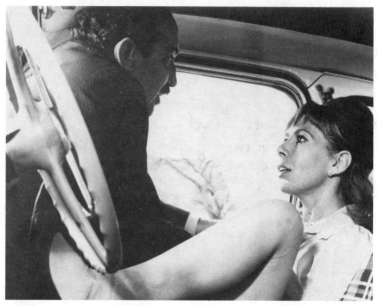

Antonio Gamero and Cristina S. Pascual in Kargus (1981),
co-directed by Juan Miñón and Miguel Angel Trujillo.

hears about the great multimillionaire intellectual Kargus
who intends to visit Madrid. The writer decides to compose
several fictional tales to relate to him, each one representative of a decade of Spanish history, in the hope of selling
them. Kargus never arrives. The writer despairs, throws
away his manuscript and strolls in Madrid's Retiro Park.
There he meets his girlfriend again and we assume that they
take up their romance where it left off. Their romance
serves as a link between the 1980s and all the tales from the
1930s on. The episodes in the film, interesting in themselves, are generally about survival: survival during the
Civil War, scavenging for food during World War II, a boy's
sexual coming of age and surviving his friend's machismo

comments, a satire on a woman's fight for her virginity, the
survival of "slogans" after the death of Franco and the decoding of protests, and finally, Franco's death and its effect
on a bourgeois family. Will they ever be able to live without their leader? Life goes on for everybody. All the characters somehow carry on, especially Hector Alterio as the
eraser of slogans and Patricia Adriani who struggles against
machismo.

GONZALO SUAREZ, usually a "B" filmmaker, has
come into his own recently with his first truly prestigious
film. Parranda (Binge, 1977) is a naturalistic tale with
overtones of fantasy concerning one day of adventures of three
quasi-vagabonds in Northern Spain (Asturias) who go out on
a binge and live through some disastrous consequences.

Finally, IMMANOL URIBE's films about the Spanish
Civil War, El proceso de Burgos (The Burgos Trial, 1980),
La fuga de Segovia (Escape from Segovia, 1981), and Poncho
(1982) each treat the problems of Spaniards and provide historical perspective on the years from the Civil War to today
in the realist tradition of the films of Drove, Camino or Saura.
Escape from Segovia reached New York in May of 1984 but
American critics were not impressed; they saw it as a superior prison-escape film, and nothing more.

Scene from Uribe's La fuga de Segovia (1981), in which escaped prisoners are captured by the Guardia Civil (photo
courtesy Stillman International)

With the arrival of the Juan Carlos government in 1976, many new directors came on the scene and the variety of films produced in Spain in the post-Franco years is a veritable fountain of riches, much of it untapped and yet to be explored internationally. In this section, I have chosen to highlight some twenty-five personal choices which seemed worthy of mention.

4. Producers & Critics

There are essentially three or four well-known Spanish producers who have achieved national and international prominence. They are Elías Querejeta, Carlos Saura's behind-the-scenes Svengali; Jorge Frade, producer of many commercial films; and José Luis Borau and Luis Megino, the addicts of the art-house, elitist cinema, who produce what they like and pay the piper, hoping for some commercial success along the way. A few directors, Borau among others, have founded their own production companies and write, produce and direct their films because in this way they are assured of total control over their product. Megino and Borau both feel that one of Spain's biggest problems lies in the distribution of their films. Megino especially admires the Australians for pushing their films on to the world market, and the Spanish film industry needs the same level of impetus.[3] Megino is also looking for stories with more universal themes so that Spanish films will be more accessible internationally.

The film critics in Madrid, especially Roger Mortimore of Sight & Sound, Vicente Molina-Foix of Fotogramas, and Miguel Marías of Guía del ocío, all share great enthusiasm for the newer post-Franco Spanish films but also feel a debt to the vacas sagradas, the three "B's": Bardem, Berlanga and Buñuel, and devote much attention to the elusive facts of Spanish film history which film scholars have been researching for the past twenty years. Mortimore is currently writing on the Spanish cinema of the 1930s; Molina-Foix and Marías continue to write criticism of the new Spanish cinema for their magazines but prefer to do more creative work. Molina-Foix is a poet and novelist and Marías, an essayist. These producers and critics, making and writing about Spanish films, share an artistic endeavor; it is their ultimate passion and the stuff of their daily existence.

5. <u>The Direction of Spanish Cinema, 1950-1985, and Its Future</u>

The Spanish cinema has come a long way since the early 1950s. Bardem and Berlanga began the impetus, using traditional filmmaking methods to breathe fresh air into the stagnating "white telephone" films of the 1930s and 1940s which copied Hollywood models. This team of directors examined essentially Spanish themes, one dramatically, the other comically. Bardem's later style has become jaded because of repetition, and he deals at times in a realist manner with unimportant, even decadent themes. Berlanga, meanwhile, has sharpened his wit and "black humor" and has reshaped his career, reaping the commercial success that long eluded him.

Borau, Drove, Garcí, Giménez-Rico, Olea and Picazo all follow the realist tradition begun by Bardem and Berlanga, relating stories about Spanish life that reveal the Spanish spirit and expose the demons at work in Spanish society. Borau longs to direct films abroad and universalize his thematic approach. Drove prefers to seek truth about the past in a realistic exploration of Spanish history that borders on revisionism. Garcí, like Borau, favors locales outside of Spain but resists geographical displacement for a "Spanish" reworking of classic Hollywood genres like the <u>film noir</u> and the sentimental-romantic dramas of the 1930s and <u>1940s</u>. Giménez-Rico and Olea are the practitioners and maintainers of the traditionalist, realist school of Spanish cinema, using their artistry and painterly backgrounds to make film classics of novels like Miguel Delibes' <u>Mi hijo idolatrado Sísi</u> and Pérez Galdos' <u>Tormento</u>. Although Picazo began his career filming great literary works like Unamuno's <u>La tía Tula,</u> his style of filmmaking now resembles the later "decadent" films of Bardem, and his scenarios are overburdened with scatological and psychological embroidery. Alcoriza, Franco and Martínez Lázaro share a common bond with Picazo.

Armiñan straddles the terrain between the imitators of Bardem-Berlanga and the adaptors of traditional realist novels, writing and directing screenplays with psychological significance but presenting them in a straightforward realist manner, tempered with humor and, sometimes, fantasy. Josefina Molina and Pilar Miró's later films fall into a similar category.

A passion for the documentary still exists in Spain. Camino, Chavarrí and Patino have produced some of the best ones, dealing with the Spanish Civil War and capital punishment. The Civil War theme is as pervasive in Spain as

World War II films on our American screen, and top Spanish directors like Erice, Miró and Saura deal in varied ways with the subject: Erice, poetically; Miró, graphically realistic, and Saura, lyrically and literarily nostalgic. Camino avoids Miró's attention to brutal details but he too has made nostalgic films, as has Giménez-Rico, about the Spanish war.

Since Franco's death and the apertura (opening up) of the film industry, the Catalonian directors, especially Ribas and Camino but also others like Bellmunt, Bigas Luna and Salgot, are trying to challenge Madrid and the Castilian film as the center of Spanish production, insisting on using their own Catalan language, recounting the past while proselytizing their separatist doctrine for a united Catalonia.

The experimentalists, too, since the apertura have found themselves limited audiences and are eager to test the new freedoms in Spanish cinema. Amo prefers elitist subjects, while Zulueta seeks the elusive "camp" or cult audience; both, however, are exploring in diverse styles bold subjects not seen on Spanish screens before 1976.

A new comic spirit has also invaded Spain, not exactly in the tradition of Berlanga's "black humor" but lighter and more airy, reminiscent of the youthful films of François Truffaut. Fernando Colomo and Fernando Trueba have explored the problems of today's urban youth and have made some entertaining, comically effervescent features that delight and provide audiences an escape from their problems. Bodegas' and Bermejo's films also fit neatly into this genre.

Finally, there are a few directors who simply defy categorization: Manuel Gutiérrez Aragón and Carlos Saura, for example, whose works cross and encompass so many thematic currents. Although Gutiérrez Aragón is much younger than Saura, his films are intense literary and intellectual experiences, searching for new ways to reveal character and essential Spanish problems. Saura, more prolific than Gutiérrez Aragón, displays a genius for finding new and exciting ways to please Spanish as well as international audiences. He has worked in a multiplicity of genres and, like Gutiérrez Aragón, is a director in search of the Spanish psyche, history, his own past and, perhaps, himself.

Where is the Spanish cinema headed in the 1980s? It is sad to see some of the Spanish directors yielding to the pressures of commercialism and the mass audience. But except for Manuel Summers and a few others, the directors cited in this volume are serious, intelligent, and interested in the

the artistic development of their craft and themselves. That this approach can produce commercial success is clear if one looks at the top grossing Spanish films for 1982. Top of the list was La colmena (The Beehive, 1981) based upon the novel by Camilo José Cela. Directed by Mario Camus, a director barely known abroad, including the United States, and starring two box-office champions, José Sacristán and Ana Belén, this film was a top financial grosser perhaps because the Spanish public enjoys seeing treasured literary works like Cela's 1950 novel transferred artistically to the screen.

Close behind La colmena, however, is Manuel Summers' To er mundo e güeno (Everybody Is Good, 1982), a grossly sentimental and vulgar film catering to low-brow audiences. And Cristóbal Colón, Descubridor (Columbus, the Discoverer, 1982), filmed by another artless, commercial director, Mariano Ozores, and starring Andres Pajares and Fiorella Faltoyano, takes third place among the money-making films in Spain in 1982.4 This film is another example of the Spaniard's penchant for history recreated in color on the Cinemascope screen.

It is a pity that a number of the films described in this book have not even been seen by a majority of Spanish moviegoers or by audiences elsewhere.5 Since Juan Carlos' return and the election of a Socialist government, despite an economy suffering from inflation, many more Spaniards are going to the movies. Audience attendance is decidedly on the rise. One hopes that the new moviegoers in Spain will skip the crassly commercial products in favor of the many more artistic films that reflect their glorious heritage.

N.B. As this book was going to press, Peter Besa mentioned the following new Spanish films for 1985-86 release in his article, "No Spanish Entry at Fest, Many Flock to Cannes for Sales, Promo Chores," appearing in the special 28th International Film Annual of Variety, published on May 1, 1985:

1. Jaime de Armiñan's La hora bruja (The Witching Hour).
2. Luis Garcia Berlanga's La vaquilla (The Little Bull).
3. Mario Camus' La vieja música (The Old Music).
3a. Fernando Colomo's The Knight of the Dragon
4. Manuel Gutiérrez Aragón's La noche mas hermosa (The Most Beautiful Night).
5. Oscar Ladoire's Bajo en Nicontina (Low in Nicotine).
6. Emilio Martínez Lázaro's Lulu de noche (Lulu at Night).

7. Juan Miñón's <u>Luna de agosto</u> (August Moon).
8. Basilio Martín Patino's <u>Los paraísos perdidos</u> (Lost Paradises).
9. Miguel Picazo's Extramuros (Extramurals).
10. Immanol Uribe's <u>La muerte de Mikel</u> (The Death of Mikel).

The new box office champ in Spain is Mario Camus' Los santos inocentes (The Holy Innocents), replacing Pilar Miró's 1981-82 success, El crimen de Cuenca (The Cuenca Crime). Other top grossing Spanish films in 1984 were Jaime Chavarrí's Las bicicletas son para el verano (Bicycles Are for the Summer), Pedro Costa Musté's El Caso Almería (The Almería Case), Tomas Aznar's Playboy en Paro, Montzo Armendariz' Tasio, Fernando Trueba's Sal Gorda, and other commercial successes were José Luis Borau's Río Abajo (On the Line), awaiting release in the U.S.A., Teo Escamilla's (cameraman turned director) Tú solo (You Alone), Carlo Suarez' El jardín secreto (The Secret Garden), Gonzalo Suarez' Epílogo (Epilogue) and Manolo Summers' La Biblia en Pasta.

Other minor successes in Spain and abroad during 1984 were Vincente Aranda's Fanny Pelopoja, Pedro Olea's Akelarre, Carlos Saura's Los Zancos (Stilts) and Pedro Almódovar's ¿Qué he hecho para merecer esto? (What Have I Done to Deserve This?), which was released in New York in late April, 1985.

Bibliography

1.

Alcoriza

Castro, Antonio. "Entrevista con L. Alcoriza y Tac-tac." Dirigido por No. 90, 44-47.

Bodegas (b. Madrid, 1933)

Besa, Peter. "Review of Los nuevos españoles." Variety (Jan. 15, 1975), 26.
Besa, Peter. "Review of Corazones de papel." Variety (Sept. 1, 1982), 19.

Bellmunt

Besa, Peter. "Review of La quinta del porro." Variety (Mar. 11, 1981), 17.

Ordóñez, Marcos. "Entrevista con F. Bellmunt." Dirigido
por No. 79, 42.

Bigas Luna (b. Barcelona, 1946)

Albero, Lluis M. "Entrevista con Bigas Luna." Dirigido
por (Sept. 1976), 18-25.
Besa, Peter. "Review of Bilbao." Variety (May. 24, 1978),
38.
Besa, Peter. "Review of Caniche." Variety (May 16, 1979),
44.
Besa, Peter. "Review of Reborn." Variety (Oct. 21, 1981),
26.

Bermejo

Besa, Peter. "Review of Vecinos." Variety (Aug. 19, 1981),
20.
Marías, Miguel. "Review of Vecinos." Casablanca (Sept.
9, 1981), 50, 52.

Franco (b. Madrid, 1949)

Balagué, Carlos. "Entrevista con Ricardo Franco." Dirigido
por (Oct. 1976), 12-15.
Besa, Peter. "Review of Pascual Duarte." Variety (May 19,
1976), 23.
Besa, Peter. "Review of Los restos del naufragio." Variety
(May 31, 1978), 23.

Martínez-Lázaro (b. Madrid, 1945)

Amig. "Review of Las palabras de Max." Variety (Mar.
3, 1978), 21.
Besa, Peter. "Review of Sus años dorados." Variety (Nov.
5, 1980), 22.

Molina (b. Cordoba, 1936)

Alberich, Enrique. "Entrevista con Josefina Molina." Dirigido
por (Nov. 1981), 20-23.
"True Story of Actress and Her Husband." New York Times
(May 6, 1983), C 10.

Salgot (b. Aiguafreda, Barcelona, 1953)

Albero, Lluis M. "Entrevista con J. A. Salgot." Dirigido
por (Feb. 1981), 8-11.

Besa, Peter. "Review of Mater Amatísima." Variety (June 11, 1980), 26, 28.
Canby, Vincent. "An Autistic Child in Barcelona." New York Times (Apr. 18, 1982), 66.

Summers (b. Seville, 1935)

Besa, Peter. "Review of Mi primer pecado." Variety (May 25, 1977), 20.
Besa, Peter. "Review of To er mundo e güeno." Variety (June 30, 1982), 20.
Schwartz, Ronald. "Recent Spanish Cinema in the United States." (June 21, 1967), unpublished article.

2.

Aranda (b. Barcelona, 1926)

Besa, Peter. "Review of Asesinato en el comité central." Variety (Sept. 15, 1982), 20.

Bartolomé (b. Alicante, 1943)

Marías, M. "Review of Después de...." Casablanca (Jul-Aug. 1981), 85-86.

Betriu (b. Organa, 1940)

Besa, Peter. "Review of Plaza de diamantes." Variety (Jun. 2, 1982), 22.
Vical Estevez, M. "Review of Los fieles sirvientes." Contracampo (Sept. 15, 1980), 60-65.

Camus (b. Santander, 1935)

Besa, Peter. "Review of La colmena." Variety (Oct. 27, 1982), 22.
Besa, Peter. "Review of Los santos inocentes." Variety (May 2, 1984), 20.
Maslin, Janet. "Review: The Holy Innocents, Spanish Peasant Family." New York Times (Sept. 30, 1984), Sec. 2, 58.
Program Notes: New York Film Festival at Lincoln Center, Sept. 29, 1984. Film was Spain's official entry in Cannes Film Festival in May and actors Alfredo Landa & Francisco Rabal shared Best Acting Award.

Ladoire

Marinero, R. "Review of A contratiempo." Casablanca (Apr. 16, 1982), 50-51.

3.

Almodóvar

Besa, Peter. "Review of Laberinto de pasiones." Variety
(Oct. 6, 1982), 18
Besa, Peter. "Review of Entre tinieblas." Variety (May
23, 1984), 23.
Besa, Peter. "Review of ¿Qué he hecho para merecer
esto? (What Have I Done to Deserve This?) Variety (Aug.
29, 1984), 23.

Betancor (b. San Cruz de Tenerife, 1944)

Besa, Peter. "Review of Valentina." Variety (June 2, 1982),
22.
Besa, Peter. "Review of 1919." Variety (Sept. 7, 1983),
24.
Maslin, Janet. "Review of Valentina." New York Times
(Aug. 5, 1983), C 15.

Gutiérrez (b. León, 1933)

Besa, Peter. "Review of Arriba Hazaña." Variety (June
21, 1978), 23.

Herralde (b. Barcelona, 1949)

Besa, Peter. "Review of Raza, el espíritu de Franco."
Variety (Nov. 23, 1977), 19.
Besa, Peter. "Review of Ultimas tardes con Teresa."
Variety (Apr. 23, 1984), 18.

Suárez (b. 1934)

Besa, Peter. "Review of Parranda." Variety (Mar. 17,
1977), 22.

Ungria (b. Madrid, 1946)

Besa, Peter. "Review of Soldados." Variety (Jan. 17, 1977),
21.

Uribe

Besa, Peter. "Review of La fuga de Segovia." Variety
(Oct. 21, 1981), 27.

Gonzales, B. "Review of El proceso de Burgos." Cinema 2002 (May 1980), 28-29.

Haun, Harry. "Review of Escape from Segovia." Daily News (June 6, 1984), n. p.

Maslin, Janet. "Review of Film: Basque, Escape from Segovia." New York Times (June 6, 1984), C 18.

Sarris, Andrew. "Review of Escape from Segovia." Village Voice (June 12, 1984), 48.

Miñón (b. Madrid, 1953) and Trujillo (b. Madrid, 1948)

Besa, Peter. "Review of Kargus." Variety (July 1, 1981), 16.

Afterword

LUIS BUÑUEL (1900-1983)

No book on Spanish film directors would be complete without mention of the prolific career of Luis Buñuel. Buñuel has had much critical exposure internationally because of the great variety of his films, beginning in the late 1920s with the surrealistic Le chien andalou (The Andalusian Dog, 1929) and ending with That Obscure Object of Desire in 1977.

He was born in Calanda (Teruel), Spain in 1900, and his career was nurtured in Spain, Mexico and France. The best four volumes about his work available in English are Freddy Buache's The Cinema of Luis Buñuel (1970), Ado Kyrou's Luis Buñuel: An Introduction (1963), the recently translated Luis Buñuel: A Critical Biography by Francisco Aranda (1976), and Virgina Higginbotham's Luis Buñuel (1979), a study of his life and films. But to really know Buñuel himself, one should read his recently published autobiography, Mi último suspiro (My Last Sigh, 1982), written in collaboration with his favorite screenwriter, Jean Claude Carrière.

Of all his films, my personal favorites are Le chien andalou (1929), Los olvidados (1950), Viridiana (1961), Tristana (1969), and finally, The Discreet Charm of the Bourgeoisie (1972). In making these films Buñuel traversed the globe from France to Mexico to Spain and finally back to France and on to Mexico, where he died on July 30, 1983. Becoming old was his principal fear. Buñuel was not afraid to die. "I must know whose fingers will close my eyes." Buñuel's spirit lives on for all Spanish film directors, and in Spain forever.

Bibliography

Broyard, Anatole. "Review of Luis Buñuel's My Last Sigh." New York Times (Sept. 28, 1983), C 4.

Canby, Vincent. "Review of film: A Short Confession by Luis Buñuel." New York Times (Jan. 23, 1985), C 14.

Flint, Peter B. "Luis Buñuel Dies at 83." New York Times (July 30, 1983), 7.

CHAPTER NOTES

Introduction

1. "Spanish Cinema," Press Release of the American Film Institute, Spanish Journal, 6, No. 1 (July 23-30, 1980), 1.

2. Idem.

3. Roger Mortimore, "Reporting from Madrid," Sight & Sound 49, 3 (Summer 1980), 156.

4. Idem.

Chapter 1

1. Interview with the director, Madrid, July 9, 1981.

2. Idem.

3. Roger Mortimore, "Reporting from Madrid," Sight & Sound 49, 3 (Summer 1980), 157.

4. Idem.

Chapter 2

1. Interview with the director, Madrid, July 18, 1982.

2. Idem.

3. Kathleen Carroll, "Review of El nido," Daily News (Aug. 9, 1982), 35.

4. Vincent Canby, "Widower and Girl in The Nest," New York Times (Aug. 10, 1982), 42.

5. Idem.

Chapter 3

1. George Sadoul, Dictionary of Filmmakers (Berkeley: Univ. of California Press, 1972), p. 15.

2. Idem.

3. Idem.

4. "Police of Madrid Free Film Director," New York Times (Feb. 23, 1956).

5. "Spain Frees Jailed Helmer Bardem," Variety (May 19, 1976).

6. "Twenty-one Classics: A Gift from Janus Films," Press Release, Museum of Modern Art (1975).

7. Pauline Kael, 5001 Nights at the Movies (New York: Scribner, 1982) p. 140.

Chapter 4

1. José Luis Guarner, "Five Directors of the Year 1981," Film Guide: 1981 (London: Tantivy Press, 1982), p. 21.

2. Program Notes from British Film Institute Festival of Cinema, London, 1981.

3. Interview with Berlanga on July 1, 1981 at the Filmoteca Nacional.

4. Interview with Berlanga at his home in Somosaguas (Madrid), July 4, 1981.

5. Interview with Berlanga at the Filmoteca Nacional, Aug. 3, 1982.

6. Interview with Berlanga at his home, July 4, 1981.

7. Idem.

8. George Sadoul, Dictionary of Filmmakers (Berkeley: Univ. of California Press, 1972), p. 21.

9. Guarner, p. 21.

10. Robert Salmaggi, "Review of Not on Your Life," New York Times (Mar. 30, 1965), 22.

11. Interview at Filmoteca Nacional, Aug. 3, 1982.

12. Andrew Sarris, "Reporting from Cannes--1982," Village Voice (May 25, 1982), 47.

13. Interview with Berlanga at the Filmoteca Nacional, Aug. 3, 1982.

14. Peter Besa, "Review of National Shotgun," Variety (May 10, 1978), 27.

15. Vicente Molina-Foix, "Notes to British Film Institute Retrospective of Spanish Cinema," British Film Institute Monograph (London: B. F. I., 1981), p. 30.

Chapter 5

1. Interview with Borau in Madrid on July 2, 1981.

2. Pressbook for Furtivos, courtesy El Imán, S. A.

3. Press Release from Swedish Film Institute, Vol I, No. 15, Oct. 1979, p. 1.

4. Interview with J. L. Borau in New York City (Hotel Mayflower) on Sept. 14, 1980.

5. Interview with Borau in Madrid, July 2, 1981.

6. Idem.

7. Interview in New York, Sept. 14, 1980.

8. Idem.

9. Vincente Molina-Foix, New Cinema in Spain (London: British Film Institute Monograph, 1977), p. 30.

10. Tom Buckley, "At the Movies," New York Times (Mar. 17, 1978), 44.

11. Janet Maslin, "Review of Furtivos," New York Times (Mar. 7, 1978), 44.

12. Tom Allen, "Review of Furtivos," Village Voice (Mar. 13, 1978), 59.

13. Roger Mortimore, "Reporting from Madrid," Sight & Sound (Summer 1980), 157.

14. Idem.

15. The May 4, 1983 issue of Variety on p. 410 reports the film is completed and now stars David Carradine, Victoria Abril and Scott Wilson. Note these interesting cast changes.

Chapter 6

1. Peter Besa, "Review of Las largas/vacaciones del 36." Variety (Apr. 21, 1976), 23.

2. Vicente Molina-Foix, New Cinema in Spain (London: British Film Institute Monograph, 1977), p. 31.

3. Interview with Jaime Camino on Aug. 4, 1982, Madrid.

Chapter 7

1. Pressbook for Estoy en crísis, courtesy of the director.

2. Interview with Fernando Colomo, June 9, 1983.

3. Peter Besa, "Review of Skyline," Variety (Oct. 12, 1983), 18.

4. Vincent Canby, "Review of Skyline," New York Times (Apr. 3, 1984), C 15.

5. Press Release, Apr. 2, 1984, "New Directors/New Films Series," Museum of Modern Art.

Chapter 8

1. Interview with Jaime Chavarrí in Madrid, July 3, 1981.

2. Vicente Molina-Foix, New Cinema in Spain (London: BFI Monograph, 1977), p. 32.

3. Idem.

4. Angel A. Pérez Gómez & José L. Martínez Montalbán, Cine español 1951-1978 (Bilbao, Ed. Mensajero, 1978), p. 82.

5. Interview with Chavarrí, Madrid, July 9 and 10, 1981.

6. Idem.

7. Peter Besa, "Review of A un Dios desconocido," Variety (Sept. 28, 1977), 24.

8. Vincent Canby, "Review of To an Unknown God," New York Times (Apr. 7, 1978), C7.

9. Interview with Jaime Chavarrí, Madrid, July 3, 1981.

10. Idem.

11. Peter Besa, "Review of Las bicicletas son para el verano," Variety (Feb. 8, 1984), 20.

Chapter 9

1. Interview with Antonio Drove, Madrid, July 9, 1981.

2. Idem.

3. Roger Mortimore, "Reporting from Madrid," Sight & Sound (Summer 1980), 157.

4. Ibid., p. 158.

Chapter 10

1. Vicente Molina-Foix, New Cinema in Spain (London: BFI Monograph, 1977), p. 34.

2. See screenplay by Angel Fernández Santos & Victor Erice, El espíritu de la colmena (Madrid: Ed. Elías Querejeta, 1976), 165 pages.

3. Press Book, Chicago Film Festival, 1973.

4. Vincent Canby, "A Perilous Country," New York Times (Sept. 24, 1976), C8.

5. A. Soriano, "Review of The Spirit of the Beehive," Sight & Sound (Winter 1973-74), 78.

6. Idem.

7. Canby, p. C8.

8. Interview with Victor Erice, Madrid, July 4, 1981.

9. Molina-Foix, p. 34.

10. Interview with Erice.

11. Press Release, "The Thirteenth International Critic Week, Los Angeles Film Exposition," Nov. 1-16, 1974, Introduction.

12. Peter Besa, "Review of El sur," Variety (June 1, 1983), 18.

Chapter 11

1. Interview with José Luis Garcí, Madrid, July 28, 1982.

2. Idem.

3. Idem.

4. Press Book for El crack, courtesy of the director.

5. Press Book for Las verdes praderas, courtesy of the director.

6. Peter Besa, "Review of El Crack," Variety (Apr. 22, 1981), 26.

7. Peter Besa, "Review of Volver a empezar," Variety (Apr. 14, 1982), 18.

8. Interview with José Luis Garcí, Madrid, July 28, 1982.

9. Peter Besa, "Review of El Crack Dos," Variety (Aug. 31, 1983), 18.

Chapter 12

1. Interview with Antonio Giménez-Rico, Madrid, July 27, 1982.

2. Idem.

3. Idem.

4. Idem.

5. See Ronald Schwartz, José María Gironella (New York: Twayne, 1972), 200 pages, for a plot summary of Gironella's entire Civil War pentology.

6. Interview with Antonio Giménez-Rico, Madrid, July 27, 1982.

7. Peter Besa, "Review of Vestida de azul," Variety (Oct. 12, 1983), 29.

Chapter 13

1. Taken from a press release given to me by the director, author unknown.

2. Interview with Manuel Gutiérrez Aragón, Madrid, July 22, 1982.

3. Idem.

4. Peter Besa, "Review of Camada negra," Variety (May 11, 1977), 79.

5. Interview with M.G. Aragón, Aug. 2, 1982.

6. Cited by Juan P. Millián in a pamphlet, "Films by M.G. Aragón," no date or publisher indicated.

7. Carlos Boyero is cited in a press release for Maravillas, no date or author specified.

8. Archer Winsten, "Spanish 'Demons' Burns with Intensity," New York Post (Mar. 2, 1984), 53.

Chapter 14

1. Vicente Molina-Foix, New Cinema in Spain (London: BFI, 1977), p. 37.

2. Ibid., p. 38.

3. Interview with Pilar Miró in Madrid, July 7, 1981.

4. J. L. Guarner, "Spain," International Film Guide 1982 (London: Tantivy, 1981), p. 269.

5. Idem.

6. Interview with Pilar Miró, Madrid, July 7, 1981.

7. "Spain Lifts Age Barriers to Pix: Tags 'Suggested,' " Variety (Aug. 3, 1983), 33.

Chapter 15

1. Interview with Pedro Olea, Madrid, July 7, 1981.

2. Idem.

3. Press Book of La casa sin fronteras, courtesy of the director.

4. Interview with the director.

5. Idem.

6. Peter Besa, "Review of Tormento," Variety (Sept. 25, 1974), 16, 18.

7. In a recent film note about Spain in Variety, Sept. 8, 1980, Pedro Olea was supposedly filming a scenario entitled Goodbye, Tony, about the lives of "call girls" in Madrid. There have been no subsequent reviews of this film, if it ever reached completion.

Chapter 16

1. Interview with Basilio Martín Patino, Madrid, July 5, 1981.

2. Idem.

3. Vicente Molina-Foix, New Spanish Cinema (London: B. F. I., 1977), p. 39.

4. James Markham, "Movies in Spain Starting to Deal with with Civil War," New York Times (Nov. 28, 1976), 15.

5. Peter Besa, "Rebirth for Helmer Patino Condemned Under Franco," Variety (Jan. 12, 1977), 64.

6. Interview with Patino, Madrid, July 5, 1981.

7. Idem.

8. Idem.

9. Interview with Patino, Madrid, July 5, 1981.

10. Idem.

11. Markham, p. 15.

12. Interview with Patino, Madrid, July 5, 1981.

Chapter 17

1. Interview with Picazo, Madrid, July 23, 1982.

2. Vicente Molina-Foix, New Cinema in Spain (London: B. F. I., 1977), 40.

3. Judith Crist, "Review of La tía Tula," Herald-Tribune (June 3, 1965), 42.

4. Robe, "Review of La tía Tula," Variety (Apr. 28, 1965), 22.

5. Interview with Picazo.

6. Idem.

Chapter 18

1. Vicente Molina-Foix, New Cinema in Spain (London: B. F. I., 1977), 42.

2. Peter Besa, "Review of La ciudad quemada," Variety (Oct. 27, 1976), 28.

3. Letter from Antoni Ribas to Ronald Schwartz, August 10, 1982.

Chapter 19

1. Interview with Roger Mortimore, Madrid, July 30, 1982.

2. "Carlos Saura," Current Biography (New York: H. W. Wilson, 1979), p. 357.

3. Vicente Molina-Foix, New Cinema in Spain (London: B. F. I., 1977), 43.

4. Interview with Vicente Molina-Foix, Madrid, July 19, 1981.

5. Gail Bartholomew, The Films of Carlos Saura, M. A. thesis, Northwestern University, 1982. Chapter on La Madriguera.

6. "Carlos Saura," Current Biography, p. 359.

7. Gail Bartholomew, Conclusion.

8. Molina-Foix, p. 43.

9. Interview with Gail Bartholomew, Madrid, Aug. 7, 1982.

10. "Carlos Saura," Current Biography, p. 360.

11. Museum of Modern Art Press Release on Deprisa, deprisa. Undated.

12. Interview with Gail Bartholomew, Madrid, Aug. 7, 1982.

13. Pauline Kael, "Review of Dulces horas," Taking It All In, (New York: Holt, Rinehart & Winston, 1984), p. 409-411.

14. Jack Kroll, "Dance of Death," Newsweek (Nov. 9, 1981), 64.

Chapter 20

1. Interview with Fernando Trueba, Madrid, July 6, 1981.

2. Idem.

3. Idem.

4. Idem.

5. Vincent Canby, "Review of Opera prima," New York Times (Jan. 6, 1982), C17.

6. Peter Besa, "Review of Opera prima," Variety (June 25, 1980), 21.

7. Interview with Trueba, July 6, 1981.

8. The May 4, 1983 issue of Variety reported that Trueba's new documentary film, Chicho, stars José Antonio Sánchez Ferlosio and will be seen in Cannes.

Chapter 21

1. Interview with José Luis Borau, Madrid, July 3, 1981, Zulueta's producer.

2. Peter Besa, "Review of Arrebato," Variety (Oct. 15, 1980), 24.

Conclusion

1. Press Release, La colmena, New York Festival of Spanish Films, Nov. 11, 1983, p. 2.

2. Herralde also made a realistic film based on Juan Marsé's novel and entitled Las últimas tardes con Teresa (Last Afternoons with Teresa, 1982), which received fairly successful reviews in Madrid.

3. Interview with Luis G. Megino, Madrid, August 2, 1982.

4. Cited from Variety's Special Issue on Cannes, May 4, 1983, p. 406.

5. A propos of commercialism the best Spanish films at the Spanish Film Festival in New York, 1983 only grossed $86,000 in three weeks, compared to $20 million for Clint Eastwood's Sudden Impact in its first ten days of release in New York and elsewhere during the same time period.

SELECTED BIBLIOGRAPHY

1. General Works

Alcover, N. & Pérez Gómez, Angel. Hallazgos, falacias y mixtificaciones del cine de los '70. Bilbao: Ed. Mensajero, 1975.

Caparrós-Lera, José María. El cine de los años setenta. Pamplona: Ed. EUNSA, 1976.

_____. El cine político. Barcelona: Ed. Dopesa, 1978.

_____. Travelling por el cine contemporáneo. Madrid: Ed. Rialp, 1981.

Castro, Antonio. El cine español en el banquillo. Valencia: Ed. Fernando Torres, 1974.

Cine español: 1980-1981. Madrid: Ed. Edagraf, 1982.

Cine para leer. Bilbao: Ed. Mensajero, 1972-1983. 12 volumes.

Galan, Diego. Venturas y desventuras de la prima Angélica. Valencia: Ed. Fernando Torres, 1974.

Gómez Mesa, Luis. La literatura española en el cine español. Madrid: Ed. Filmoteca Nacional de España, 1978.

Gubern, Román. Homenaje a Carlos Saura. Madrid: Ed. Huelva, 1979.

Hernández-Les, Juan & Gato, Miguel. El cine de autor en España. Madrid: Ed. Castalia, 1978.

International Film Guide: 1964-1984. London: Tantivy Press, 1964-1984. 21 vols.

Larraz, Emmanual. El cine español. Paris: Ed. Masson et Cie., 1973.

Martínez Torres, Augusto. Cine español: años sesenta. Barcelona: Ed. Anagrama, 1973.

Pérez Gómez, Angel A. & Martínez Montalbán, José L. Cine español 1951-1978. Bilbao: Ed. Vizcaína, 1979.

Pérez Merinero, Carlos y David. Cine español. Una reinterpretación. Barcelona: Ed. Anagrama, 1976.

Santolaya, Ernesto. Luis G. Berlanga. Ed. Victoria: Filmoteca Nacional, 1979.

Torres, Augusto M. Cine español, años sesenta. Barcelona: Ed. Anagrama, 1973.

Villegas López, Manuel. El nuevo cine español. San Sebastián: XV Festival Internacional del Cine, 1967.

Vizcaíno-Casas, Fernando. Diccionario del cine español. Madrid: Ed. Nacional, 1967.

_____. Historia y anecdota del cine español. Madrid: Ed. Adra, 1976.

2. Monographs

Kovács, Katherine S. Editor. "New Spanish Cinema." Quarterly Review of Film Studies, Vol 8, No. 2 (Spring 1983), 1-103.

Molina-Foix, Vicente. New Cinema in Spain. London: British Film Institute Monograph, 1977, 55 pages.

3. Articles

Arata, Luis O. "I Am Ana: The Play of the Imagination in The Spirit of the Beehive." Quarterly Review of Film Studies, (Spring 1983), 27-34.

Borau, José Luis. "Without Weapons." Quarterly Review of Film Studies, (Spring 1983), 85-90.

D'Lugo, Marvin. "Carlos Saura: Constructive Imagination

in Post-Franco Cinema." Quarterly Review of Film Studies, (Spring 1983), 35-48.

Eder, Richard. "Post-Franco Films Seek Own Identity." New York Times, (Jan. 22, 1980), C 7.

García Ray, Antonio. "La decada de los setenta en el cinematográfo español." Cinema 2002, (Mar.-Apr. 1980), 22-28.

Goytisolo, Juan. "Algunas consideraciones respecto al cine español." Cine cubaño, Año 3, No. 10 (1963), 12-15.

Gubern, Román. "Tendencies, Genres and Problems of Spanish Cinema in the Post-Franco Period." Quarterly of Film Studies, Vol. 8, No. 2 (Spring 1983), 15-26.

Insdorf, Annette. "Spain Also Rises," Film Comment, 16 No. 4 (July-Aug. 1980), 13-17.

_____. "Soñar con tus ojos: Carlos Saura's Melodic Cinema." Quarterly Review of Film Studies, (Spring 1983), 49-56.

Kinder, Marsha. "The Children of Franco in the New Spanish Cinema." Quarterly Review of Film Studies, (Spring 1983), 57-76.

Kovâcs, Katherine S. "Introduction: Background on the New Spanish Cinema." Quarterly Review of Film Studies, (Spring 1983), 1-6.

_____. "Berlanga Life Size." (Interview) Quarterly Review of Film Studies, (Spring 1983), 7-14.

_____. "The Last Word." (Book Review of Buñuel's Autobiography Mon dernier soupir.) Quarterly Review of Film Studies, (Spring 1983), 95-97.

Marías, Miguel. "José Luis Borau: El Francotirador Responsable." Dirigido por, (Sept. 1975), 20-25.

Mortimore, Rober. "Spain: Out of the Past." Sight & Sound, (Autumn 1974), 199-202.

_____. "Reporting from Madrid." Sight & Sound, (Summer 1980), 156-158.

Paranagua, Pablo Antonio. "Espagne: desencanto." Positif, No. 240 (Mars 1981), 41-47.

_____. "Le premier congrès démocratique du cinéma espagnol." Positif, No. 246 (Sept. 1981), 43-49.

_____. "Solitudes espagnoles." Positif, No. 260 (Oct. 1982), 51-52.

Rawson, Wade. "Spanish Film Now: A Primer." Press Release, August 1984, distributed by Kino International Corporation, 9 pages.

Riambau, Esteve. "Cine español 78/80; Testimonio de una crisis." Dirigido por, (Aug. 1980), 31-35.

Shickel, Richard. "Spanish Film: Paradoxes and Hopes." Harper's (Sept. 1967), 127-129.

Vargas Llosa, Mario. "Furtivos." Quarterly Review of Film Studies, Vol. 8, No. 2 (Spring 1983), 77-84.

"Spanish Film Festival in New York." New York Times, (Nov. 11, 1983), III, 8.

4. Reference

Alvarez, Max Joseph. Index to motion pictures reviewed by Variety: 1907-1980. Metuchen, N.J.: Scarecrow Press, 1982, 510 pages.

INDEX OF FILM TITLES

(Underscores indicate pages with photographs)

INDEX OF DIRECTORS, PRODUCERS, AND CRITICS

(Underscores indicate pages with photographs)

N.B.: This index was programmed and supervised by Dr. Michael Rosson, Head, Media Center at Kingsborough College (CUNY), whose aid was invaluable.